W9-DIS-260

AIRBORNE

AIRBORNE

Assault from the Sky

Hans Halberstadt

Presidio Press ★ Novato, California
THE PRESIDIO POWER SERIES
LANDPOWER #3001

Copyright © 1988 by Hans Halberstadt
Published by Presidio Press
31 Pamaron Way, Novato, CA 94949

All rights reserved. No part of this book may be reproduced or utilized in any form or by any means, electronic or mechanical, including photocopying, recording or by any information storage and retrieval systems, without permission in writing from the Publisher. Inquiries should be addressed to Presidio Press, 31 Pamaron Way, Novato, CA 94949.

Library of Congress Cataloging-in-Publication Data

Halberstadt, Hans.
    Airborne: assault from the sky.

    (Presidio power series. Landpower book; #3001)
    1. United States. Army—Parachute troops—History.
I. Title.   II. Series.
UD483.H35   1988   356′.166′0973   87-16878
ISBN 0-89141-279-4 (pbk.)

All photographs copyright © Hans Halberstadt, with the exception of those on pages 11, 23, 24-25, 27, 28, and 30, which were provided courtesy of the 82nd Airborne Historical Museum.
Photo on page 127 (bottom) courtesy of SSG Kirk Wyckoff

Printed and bound in the United States of America.

Contents

Acknowledgements

One name goes on the title page but many names build a book. I want to render honors to my beloved co-conspirators, particularly the people at Presidio Press: Joan Griffin, Lynn Dragonette, and the Kane dynasty for inventing this singular series of documentary portraits.

At the United States Army Basic Airborne course, Lieutenant Colonel Scott, and all the Black Hats for their tolerance and insight — as well as for letting me jump from the tower. Thanks also to the Fort Benning Public Affairs shop for baby-sitting me for a week.

The 82nd Airborne Division provided tremendous support for this book. Special thanks to Maj. Garner M. Nason, the division's straight-shooting spokesman, and his faithful Indian companions, Sergeants Cole, Wykoff, and Oleski, as well as Lieutenant Herrel. We are also endebted to Dr. John DuVall and the 82nd Airborne Historical Museum for much cooperation and assistance with text and photographs.

Several units within the division were particularly helpful: Company A, 2nd Battalion, 325th Airborne Infantry Regiment; Alpha Battery, 1st Battalion, 319th Airborne Artillery Regiment. Thanks go to Captains Nicholson, Anderson, and Pence; to Lt. Tom Oblack for many insights; to many others who — despite what I told them about being from the *National Enquirer* — were open and candid about the institution in which they serve. Thanks also to 3rd Battalion, 12th Special Forces Group (Airborne) for teaching me all I needed to know — and more — about the gentle art of jumpmastering.

I must also salute two partners: my wife, April, for putting up with a lot of silliness; and Vera Williams, who is my most critical critic.

And special thanks to Lt. Ralph Kirk Henry, Airborne Ranger, for his wit and wisdom, hospitality, and unfailing good cheer while dragging me around diverse drop zones, ranges, tactical operations centers, helicopters, aircraft, and saloons. To him and the many others like him, I say — "AIRBORNE!"

First Lieutenant Ralph Kirk Henry, Airborne Ranger, the 82nd Airborne Division's tactical Assistant Public Affairs Officer, on Sicily Drop Zone on day one of Operation Market Time.

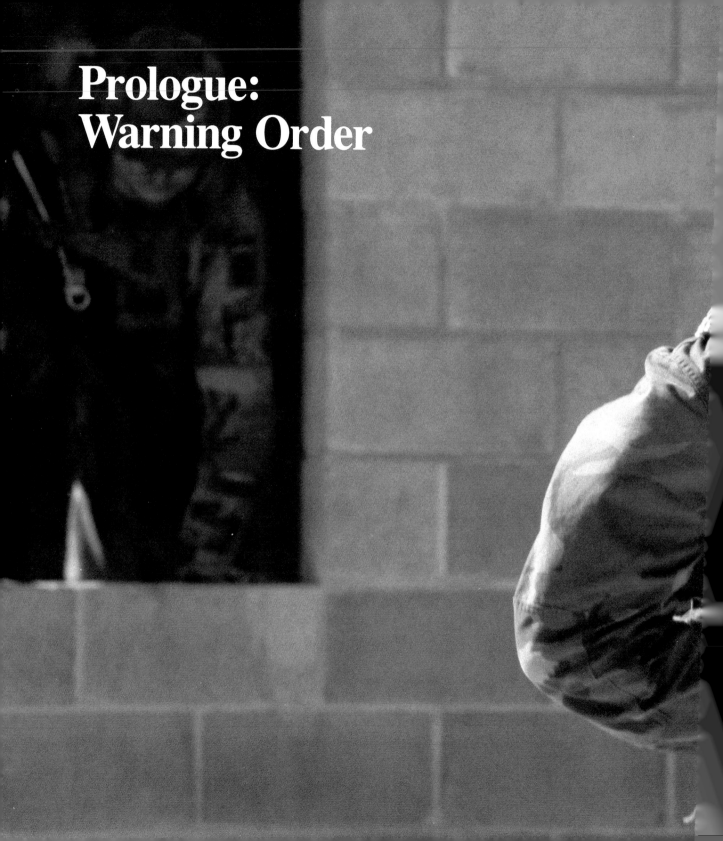

Prologue:
Warning Order

Considering the amount of fantasy, treasure, and blood that our society invests in its defense, it is curious how little most of us know about our defenders. This book, like the others in the series of POWER books, is a documentary portrait of an organization and institution within the vast realm of what the media calls the defense establishment. That establishment, as presented on the evening news, in movies like *Top Gun* or *Rambo,* is a peculiar form of fantasy, designed by and for people alien to the contemporary military. It is a misleading fantasy, sometimes flattering, sometimes hostile, that can make the people and the weapons of the combined arms team seem to be more or less than they are. The military institution is often mentioned in films, on television, in newspapers and magazines; it is mentioned so often that we tend to assume we understand how it works. The consequence is that (for most of us) our impression is based on a kind of lie, one which many in the military intensely resent, but are prohibited from refuting because of their role as servants of the government. A consequence of having a free press in a democracy is that people can publish just about anything.

These books have a different scope and intent. They are in-depth studies of components of the military, and are researched from within the units and activities they describe, from the cockpits and on the ground. They are portraits of organizations with tremendous national and international significance, from the point of view of the people within them. For those of us who construct these portraits, the reality is infinitely more fascinating than the fiction. The American airborne today is a dramatic, important part of the defense of the country, with enough heritage and high theater for anybody.

Our focus in these volumes is different than that of most in the genre. Most books about military subjects are chronologies of significant battles and campaigns, from the point of view of the generals and senior commanders. The POWER books, on the other hand, are based on the premise that generals don't win battles; privates and sergeants and lieutenants do, and it is their story we try to tell. We are interested in the individuals—their characters, education, and work. The military is a massive institution of people interacting in complex ways. At times they are tasked with defending us and shedding a great deal of blood in the process, their own as well as that of enemies.

Who is this person we call a soldier? In war or peace, the military is a kind of "calling," like the priesthood, which appeals to some and repulses others. It is a life of service and sacrifice. We refer to soldiers as "being in the service." It is a life of apartness, within a closed and cloistered society. There is an admission ritual, which begins with an oath; then the material links with normal society are stripped away. A soldier accepts a life of relative poverty and relative chastity (although not by choice), of hardships that may be quite extreme. His clothes proclaim him as special and apart from common society. Both soldier and priest are concerned with vice and virtue in life; the weapons are different, and the attitudes toward life are different, but there is a moral point of

Previous pages: An M60 gunner makes his move across the open area at the MOUT (Military Operation and Urban Terrain) site at Fort Bragg in a rehearsal for an exercise in urban combat. *Right:* The foundation of the army: an infantry squad from A Company, 2nd Battalion, 325th Airborne Infantry Regiment, 82nd Airborne Division.

Old soldier, combat soldier: General John Foss, 18th Airborne Corps commander at the time this picture was made.

Two mid-level managers pause in their routine in the field; the noncommissioned officers are the real leaders of the army in war and peace.

departure for both professions. Every soldier knows, however, when he raises his right hand and swears the oath of enlistment, that he commits himself to mortal sacrifice and violent death if required.

This volume describes the contemporary airborne infantry, the so-called paratroopers of legend. It is a fairly fresh legend as legends go, only about forty-five years old. But the legend and its heirs, the contemporary airborne, are a vital part of the army today. They established their character almost as soon as they were organized in the early forties. The kids who survived the jumps into Italy, France, and Holland are old men now, but they are honored on a daily basis by their military heirs. Jump wings are as difficult to earn today as they were two generations ago, and they mean as much. Twenty-two thousand men and a few hundred women spend three weeks earning them every year. Most never serve in an airborne unit or earn jump pay. But they wear their wings just above the "U.S. Army" tape on their uniforms as a proclamation. There is the "leg" army and the airborne army, and there isn't any argument about who is "high speed/low drag." The airborne is where the foundations of American infantry virtue are maintained, to the benefit of those within and without the airborne. It is only the entry point to the contemporary American versions of the samurai, the soldier who combined physical, mental, and moral qualities and developed them all into a coherent and overpowering spirit, irresistible in battle. Jump wings don't get you into these societies, merely to the front gate, where you have far more to prove.

The airborne of today fits into a huge and complicated system of military tactics and technologies; it is profoundly different than those that existed in 1941, when the American airborne was developed. The way we maintain our military is different than ever before in American history. Our weapons frighten even those who operate them. Things can happen so quickly in our world, that to have any realistic chance of affecting those events, we must maintain huge forces on continuous alert. Our enemies of 1945, Germany and Japan, are close allies now, good friends and equal partners; the Soviets, with whom we defeated Germany, have become our enemies in a vague sort of war and peace. The concept of conflict has been warped and tangled by the development of nuclear weapons, which infect the thinking of every planner and international politician. For the first time since the American Revolution we have a professional standing army, one of the very things the founding fathers hoped to avoid.

With the demise of the draft, military service is no longer a rite of passage for most young men. The link between the whole society and the army is gone — with some advantages for the army. The quality of the people in the military today is exceedingly high, far higher than in the draft years, limited as it is to those who perceive it as a calling and as a profession. But it is an insulated profession, and very few people outside the service have any concept of the nature of airborne war or airborne warriors.

At its foundation, this book is about war and warfare, and both involve the quite distasteful occupation of slaying other human beings. I provide this reminder because it is easy to be seduced by the drama of the people, equipment, and activities portrayed in this book, which is written during a time of what passes for peace. Despite the smiling faces and the sexy aircraft, the daring and courage of these wonderful young men, there

6

is something extremely serious and frightening about the topic, because these young men understand that they are at high risk. They know what the odds are going to be when push comes to shove in a real shoot-out. They talk about it, think about it, plan for it. Although they are all intensely alive, it is part of their profession to think often of death.

Elements of a squad move forward. The rifleman becomes the security element, while behind him one of the members of the squad moves up. Then it will be the rifleman's turn to maneuver while his associate protects him.

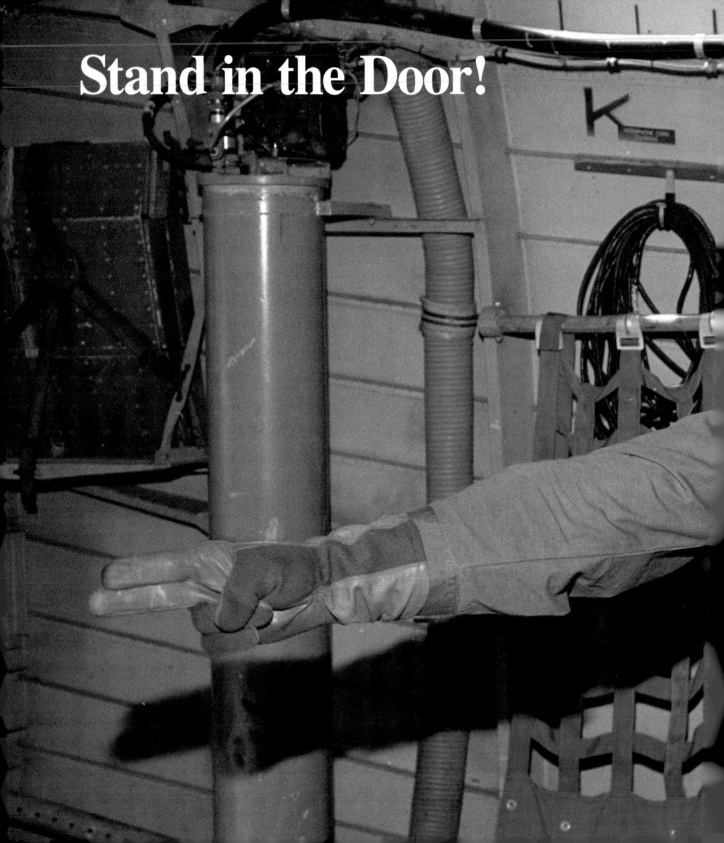

"GET READY!" is the first command. The jumpmaster has to yell it over the noise of the aircraft; he gestures powerfully with both hands toward the stick of jumpers and slams one boot on the deck, all in one practiced movement, demanding the complete attention of the jumpers.

"GET READY!" is their response, shouted as a chorus by every man in the dark airplane. The jumpers are ready and have been for weeks. But the routine is that they poise themselves on the edge of their troop seats, hands on knees and eyes on the jumpmaster, wound tightly ready to spring loose. The jump light burns red by the door. It means *not yet!*

"STAND UP!" is the next command. The jumpmaster yells and also gestures the signal. "STAND UP!" is the response, shouted in chorus. The stick struggles to its collective feet. On average, they claim to carry 120 pounds of ammunition, grenades, radios, weapons, food, flashlights. One (a general) is bringing a bottle of scotch. The jump light burns red: *not yet!*

"HOOK UP!" is the command.

"HOOK UP!" the stick yells back. Each jumper is dressed in dark olive and black, each face is painted, everything that will reach the ground is camouflaged. On each olive drab parachute, however, is a bright yellow static line that will stay with the airplane when the jumper leaves. The static line terminates in a big aluminum clip. Each jumper hooks up to the cable strung along the inside of the aircraft. A pin locks the hook in the closed position on the cable. Each man on the stick grips the static line and waits.

"CHECK STATIC LINE!" Each jumper checks the static line of the man in front of him.

"CHECK EQUIPMENT!" is the command. This is just about it.

"SOUND OFF FOR EQUIPMENT CHECK!" The last man yells "OK!" and taps the man in front of him, who repeats the action until each has had his say. The first man in the stick looks the jumpmaster in the eye and yells "OK!"

"STAND IN THE DOOR!" The jumpers crowd toward the open door, waiting, watching the jumpmaster, and watching the light. The door position is a spring-loaded crouch, hands outside, eyes on the horizon. The first man stands there, ready to lead the other jumpers out into the dark.

Tracers are visible here and there across the darkened landscape, along the hostile shore. Far away the night is brightened by the light of an exploding airplane, which has been found, fixed, and destroyed by the enemy, carrying the jumpers down with it.

There are a few occasions in life when you can watch your destiny approach you, as the events of years and months and weeks and days focus down into minutes and seconds and heartbeats; then: *green light!*

"GO!"

It has been more than forty years since the invasion of Europe was led by the 101st and 82nd Airborne Divisions on the fabled night of 6 June 1944. It was a bad drop and casualties were heavy. Not as bad as the 50 percent that had been predicted, but bad enough. Nobody landed where they were supposed to and most equipment was

---

Previous pages: Sgt. Jamie Allen commands: "Stand in the door!" – the last of his commands before tapping you out.

lost in swamps that nobody had planned for. The drop should have been a total disaster.

Well, in war, and particularly in the airborne, things like this happen. It is unusual when things go as planned. American soldiers, and especially airborne soldiers, have ways of dealing with situations like this. One is humor, and they invented a word for situations like the Normandy drop, a word used frequently even today. The word is "FUBAR," and it stands for "fucked up beyond all recognition." That's the way it was in Normandy,

Eisenhower talks to members of the 101st Airborne Division just before they climbed aboard the aircraft that would take them to Normandy. Ike feared half of these men would be casualties on the DZ; it wasn't that bad, but it was bad enough.

A SAW gunner from the 82nd. The Squad Automatic Weapon provides heavy suppressive fire for the benefit of each infantry squad. But remember, in actual combat, to take the blank adapter off the muzzle!

and plenty of places before and since. FUBAR isn't a polite word, and you will not hear it often on television; but it isn't a polite business, either — the business of war and warriors.

The Normandy invasion began a crusade, and it was led by the 82nd and 101st Airborne Divisions. Although they didn't suffer as many casualties on the drop as they had expected, they suffered them soon enough. When they were finally pulled out of combat three weeks later, they were minus nearly 10,000 airborne soldiers who had been killed, wounded, or captured. But they had prevailed.

Coming off the drop zone after jumping in on Market Time, these infantrymen move toward their assembly areas. They will then spend the next two or three weeks camping and playing hide and seek.

THE AIRBORNE, THEN AND NOW

The role of airborne soldiers within the military is a curious one, based on tradition and ancient virtues. They are uncommon foot soldiers, infantry like any other infantry, but special. They may get to work by parachute, but that is where their work begins, rather than ends. The airborne is supposed to be used for special jobs—to surprise and overwhelm an enemy in a localized area, to hold ground until reinforcements arrive.

Of the five airborne divisions of 1945, only one remains a full-fledged parachute organization, and that is the 82nd Airborne Division, whose home is Fort Bragg, North Carolina. Although three of the other four divisions have been deactivated and one is now an "air-assault" division, that

The first man in the stick waits to jump. He holds the static line in a "bight" to keep it from catching on anything.

doesn't mean airborne operations have become less important. Rather, they have been adapted, and much of the work of the old airborne units has been included in the tactics of conventional infantry, thanks to helicopters and other innovations and technologies. The airborne is also sustained in many small, specialized units, like the navy's SEALs, the Ranger battalions, Special Forces, and other elite groups. The marines have the Force Recon units and the air force has Air/Sea Rescue. They are all airborne — "super-duper-para-troopers," as the Black Hats at Benning say.

The airborne is a relatively low-tech element of the whole structure of national defense, a weapon sometimes called a "triad." A triad is a three-pointed spear, and in this case, the points are air forces, sea forces, and land forces. The air force is a bright and shiny point, and an expensive one; so is the navy. Both are highly technical, very

A C-141 from Pope Air Force Base puts out a stick of jumpers over Sicily DZ. The 141 B model can jam aboard a maximum of 152 jumpers, although they better be friends, because it will be tight.

expensive, and require highly complicated planning and tactics. When good press is given out, they tend to get it. By comparison, the army is more simple, more basic, less expensive—and dressed in camouflage battle dress utilities (BDUs) instead of dress whites.

And yet, this army is the central point of the spear—the strongest, toughest part—its foundation. The navy and the air force, bottom line, exist to back up the guy on the ground—the rifleman, that uncommon foot soldier. Nobody holds ground but the soldier. Nobody else controls the things that decide world events, long term. Even in the nuclear age, the ultimate weapon isn't the cruise missile, the F-14 fighter, Trident submarines, or the ICBM. It's the "eleven-bravo," an infantryman with an M16 rifle who, when combined with friends and associates into fire teams and squads and platoons, becomes capable of some truly awesome accomplishments.

Way out on the sharp end of the central spear is 82nd Airborne Division, which, like the missiles and bombers, is ready to be launched into combat at any moment. There are 15,000 jumpers in the division, in three regiments of infantry and a number of supporting units. The chances of them going to combat are far better than the missiles that get so much attention. They are like a fire department, although their emergencies are bigger and they always fight fire with fire.

THE HISTORY OF PARACHUTING AND AIRBORNE OPS

The concept of the parachute goes back to the fifteenth century. Leonardo da Vinci, who visualized all types of military hardware in use today (including the helicopter), described and sketched a man-carrying parachute whose basic dimensions were quite close to those used today. For 300 years it was just an idea with no place to go, but then balloons were invented.

It wasn't until 1785 that someone tried to apply the concept in a practical way: a French balloonist named Jean Pierre Blanchard dropped a pet dog from several hundred feet. The dog resented the honor and left the drop zone trailing his canopy, never to be seen by Monsieur Blanchard again.

The first human jump is unrecorded, but during the early 1800s acrobats were descending from balloons using parachutes that were a combination of canopy and trapeze. These jumps were part of the exhibitions of the time. At first, the novelty of the balloon was tremendously exciting; once people overcame their fear of it, crowds paid to see one go aloft. But after a few ascents the audiences got restless and clamored for something more thrilling, preferably including a fatality. It was the Indianapolis 500 of the time. In order to maintain the size of the crowd (and the receipts at the gate), acrobats were employed to climb around on the balloon in flight and do their acts while suspended from the basket. Then (and we don't know who was the first, or when) these acrobats began dropping from the balloon under parachutes and doing their acts from the cross bars. The parachutes were rigid, tent-like affairs, tied from the apex to the basket of the balloon; when the time came to leave, a helper in the basket cut the rope and down came the acrobats under their exotic contraption.

In this era of do-it-yourself science, many unfortunate innovations were conceived and attempted. Aircraft designs were developed and tested for many decades with depressing results, until the Wright brothers finally got a plane to fly. The balloon was becoming the reliable way of traveling around in the ozone, and the acrobats' jumps provoked interest in parachutes. People felt qualified to invent just about anything, including parachutes, and in 1837 a gentleman named Robert Cocking came up with one way to get his name included in the airborne history chapter.

Cocking developed a parachute shaped like a teacup, about the same size and shape as the one we use today, except it was upside down. It looked like an inverted umbrella. This design, he felt, should control the oscillations that plagued the jumpers of his time (who had not yet discovered the virtues of an aperture at the apex). He set out to demonstrate his invention one lovely English summer day in 1837, suspended from an immense balloon named *Nassau,* piloted by Charles Green. At an altitude of about 4,000 feet, pilot Green yelled down a question novice jumpers still hear: "Are you sure you want to go through with this?" Cocking replied that he was good to go, and Green cut him loose.

The canopy was covered with linen and used stiffeners made out of thin metal tubes to retain its shape. At 223 pounds it was heavy. At first the canopy worked fine, but then the stiffening tubes started to fail, and the canopy developed a large hole. The parachute lost its shape and Cocking augered in, much to the satisfaction of the large crowd watching. They had just witnessed the first parachute fatality. Cocking's last words had been, "I've never felt so confident in my whole life!" The use of the parachute for entertainment in England promptly fell into decline, although it continued in Europe and America.

In 1884, two brothers, Samuel and Thomas Baldwin, were working on ways to spice up their circus act. They were high-wire walkers, and had often performed from trapeze bars suspended from balloons in flight. They developed a concept for the parachute somewhat similar to the one in use today, with a stowed canopy attached to a body harness by suspension lines. Until this time, parachutes were variations of the da Vinci design, using stiffeners and a rigid canopy suspended in an opened shape. The Baldwins' design used no stiffeners, just a fabric canopy that was folded up and stuffed into a container. The canopy was attached to a body harness worn by the parachutist. The container was not worn by the jumper but was attached to the balloon's rigging or basket. It took several years for the brothers to assemble a full-sized model of their design, which they tested from an altitude of 3,000 feet. The brothers weren't as ignorant as people had said; they used sandbags instead of themselves for the first drop. The parachute worked beautifully, with a good canopy appearing promptly after extraction from the container. The way was now clear for aerial delivery of sandbags.

The Baldwins decided to demonstrate their improved parachute to the public, and sold tickets for the event at Golden Gate Park in San Francisco on 30 January 1887. Thomas Baldwin, the younger brother, was elected to jump. The balloon was tethered to ensure it stayed within sight of the sellout crowd. The brothers took the balloon up to 5,000 feet; Tom climbed onto the edge of the basket, paused, then jumped. The device worked perfectly and within five seconds he was riding under a good chute. He landed safely, and interest in parachuting increased enormously. But the interest was still focused on entertainment, because there was no other application at the time.

In 1903, after many failures, the powered airplane was developed and quickly evolved into a practical device. Many lives were lost, however, when the new invention came unglued while in flight, and it wasn't long before the parachute was considered as a rescue device for pilots in trouble. A carnival jumper named Leo Stevens designed and built a container for a parachute that could fit under the wing of an airplane; the pilot wore a harness that was attached to the parachute. When the need arose, the pilot simply departed the aircraft and his weight extracted the parachute from its container. The device was demonstrated for the first time on 28 February 1912 at Jefferson Barracks, a Missouri army post, by Albert Berry. A veritable multitude of infantrymen watched from the parade ground as the airplane approached at 1,000 feet and fifty miles per hour. Berry went through his own prejump checklist, climbed down on the landing gear, and jumped. He got a good canopy and landed behind the mess hall, to the acclaim of the troops.

The event was important: containerized parachutes like this, which were also reliable and efficient when used from balloons, were utilized through the First World War. But the parachute as demonstrated wasn't practical. It took too long for the jumper to get rigged and into position for the device to be helpful in an emergency. Berry's jump got a lot of publicity, however, which inspired others to improve on the concept. Within two years came a significant improvement — the back-pack container — invented by Charles Broadwick.

His design used a harness resembling a sleeveless coat; the canopy and suspension lines were stowed on the back. The apex of the canopy was attached to a static line by a breakaway tie, and the static line ended in a small hook that the jumper connected to any available aircraft component. It was, in many ways, similar to the design used today. In April 1914, just a few months before World War I began, Broadwick was able to demonstrate his design to the U.S. Army. The chute was jumped by Broadwick's adopted daughter, Tiny, then twenty-two years old. She had been jumping from balloons since she was fifteen. She made her exit from a Curtis biplane and, by hauling on the risers like a good airborne trooper, maneuvered herself to a landing before an amazed general and his staff. The general wrote a glowing report. But the army ignored the concept, and, when American pilots flew into combat three years later, it was without parachutes.

During the Great War, balloons were used for observation, as they had been since the Civil War. Back then, balloons were fairly safe from hostile fire, being out of range of most small arms. The airplane changed that in a heartbeat, and balloons (filled, as they were, with hydrogen) began getting shot up and going down in flames. The observers aboard resented this, and soon the containerized parachutes that had provided thrills for audiences before the war were providing thrills and close escapes for the young men under the balloons. Pilots from both sides attacked the observation balloons, and as soon as one of the fighters got close, the observers prudently dived over the side. On several occasions pilots without ammunition for their guns dived on the balloons just to see the observers bail out. One American balloon observer, Lieutenant Phelps, set the record by jumping five times during 1917 and 1918; three jumps were supposed to be the limit, but Phelps was clearly Airborne/Ranger material, and stuck with it.

During the war, only Germany provided parachutes for its aircrews. They used a canopy and suspension lines stowed in a container. When it came time to depart the aircraft, they lifted the container from under the seat, stood on the seat, tossed the container over the side, then followed it. Inelegant, but functional. Pilots of all the Allied nations envied them, particularly during those endless moments while they rode their flaming aircraft into the ground.

Col. William (Billy) Mitchell, who was in charge of Allied air units, attempted to get parachutes for his aviators, without success. The army, in a longstanding tradition, decided to conduct some tests, and they were still testing when the war was concluded in 1918. But while Mitchell was thinking about the lifesaving possibilities of the parachute, he also began to think of ways it might be used as a strategic device for offensive operations. To him goes the distinction of suggesting the first airborne assault.

Mitchell later wrote about his meeting with Gen. John Pershing on 17 October 1918:

I. . .proposed to him that in the spring of 1919, when I would have a great force of bombardment planes, he should assign one of the infantry divisions permanently to the Air Service, preferably the 1st Division; that we should arm the men with a great number of machine guns and train them to go over the front in our large airplanes, which would carry ten or fifteen of these soldiers. We could equip each man with a parachute, so that when we desired to make a rear attack on the enemy, we could carry these men over the lines and drop them off at a prearranged strong point, fortify it, and we could supply them by aircraft with food and ammunition. Our low flying attack aviation would then cover every road in the vicinity, both day and night, so as to prevent the Germans falling on them before they could thoroughly organize the position. Then we could attack the Germans from the rear, aided by an attack from our army in the front, and support the whole maneuver with our great air force.

The war ended twenty-five days after the meeting. The proposal remained only an idea in the mind of a visionary who would not live to see his ideas vindicated (or his honor restored) by the events of the war that followed.

The American army didn't completely abandon development of the parachute, and in 1919 a board was established at McCook Field to determine which type of parachute was suitable for American aviators. The board was headed by Maj. E. L. Huffman, who sent letters inviting all known jumpers in the country to demonstrate equipment and techniques that might be purchased by the government.

One of the respondents was a circus performer known as "Sky High" Irvin, who had been jumping since the age of sixteen and had logged numerous jumps over the years. He presented the first free-fall parachute, a concept that required the jumper to manually activate the release of the canopy with a ripcord instead of a static line. The Irvin model used a harness instead of a coat. The canopy was thirty-two feet in diameter, with twenty-four suspension lines. Instead of being extracted by a static line, the canopy was deployed by a pilot chute that sprang from the container when the jumper pulled the ripcord. Until this time, it was believed that free-falls couldn't be tolerated by a human being, who would either be immobilized by the force of the airflow or by fear of the situation. Irvin proved them wrong by making a delayed-opening jump from 1,500 feet, which convinced the board to sign a contract with him for 300 parachutes. By 1922 a parachute was a required part of the uniform of military and airmail pilots, and the design remained virtually unchanged for the next fifty years.

After World War I, the United States essentially destroyed its military establishment overnight. What was left was a caretaker staff to run the flag up the pole at the few remaining posts. The mood of the military was conservative and thrifty in the extreme. The service was viewed by society as a profession for men who couldn't succeed elsewhere, and there were precious few opportunities for advancement for the men who stayed. Many officers remained in grade for ten or more years, waiting seventeen years or more to make first lieutenant. Eisenhower, Bradley, MacArthur, Patton, and all the other heroes of World War II endured an eternity in a kind of professional purgatory between the wars, a period filled with old men and old ideas and old weapons.

The stagnant atmosphere of the American military was missing in Europe, where the war had a profound effect on its participants, an effect that Americans didn't feel and didn't often think about. The conclusion of the First World War set the stage for the second, and preparations for new hostilities were made almost immediately following the surrender of the German forces and their allies. The Germans deeply resented the terms imposed on them and many wanted relief and revenge. The stage was set for German innovation—in secret. The Soviets had a similar situation. The revolution cut many links with the past, and it was a time of dramatic change.

The 1930s were a time of rising tensions in the world, and Germany, Italy, and Japan were polishing the contents of arsenals they would use

shortly. The Soviet armed forces began a process of modernization, which included the concept of airborne operations as a way of transporting large numbers of men into battle behind enemy lines. In the fall of 1931 an experimental parachute unit was formed with volunteers; it would be ten years before a similar effort was attempted in the United States. By 1935 battalion-sized exercises were being held, and in 1936 the Soviet Field Service Regulations said, "Parachute units are an efficient means for disorganizing the enemy's command and control, and for operations in close coordination with forces attacking from the front, the parachute units are able to exert a decisive influence on the complete defeat of the enemy in a given direction."

In 1935 the French also established a parachute training school. In 1937 Germany started a secret parachute school at Stendal, but by this time their military redevelopment was nearing maturity. The German organization retained the airborne as an element of the air force (Luftwaffe), which created a few problems after they were on the ground, but it worked. The European nations were experimenting with variations of what we would call today airborne and air assault techniques, using both parachute delivery and airlanding of men and equipment. Common to these experiments was a fascination with the parachute as a way of getting an armed force behind the lines of an adversary. The parachute and the transport aircraft both seemed to fit the job, but they were only the beginning for the men adapting these

The perils of parachuting, 1941. A member of the 501st Parachute Infantry Battalion considers his options while training at lovely Fort Benning, Georgia.

23

resources to the tactical and strategic plans of their services. How did the soldiers carry their weapons? How did they communicate? How did a commander retain control over such a force? What were the limits and the virtues of this concept?

The problems began with the parachutes and the aircraft, neither of which was designed specifically for the work for which it was now being used. Most countries used a parachute intended for simple emergency lifesaving, with a single point of connection to the harness, a D ring behind the head. This meant that the jumper had no directional control during descent and landed where the winds took him. The Germans and Japanese retained this feature right through the war. Another problem was the opening shock; in the days before deployment bags and sleeves, the canopy opened with a bang that would leave bruises and occasionally render a jumper uncon-

scious. Yet another problem was the layout of the available jump aircraft. In some cases, jumpers dropped from bomb-bay doors; in others they tried to squeeze out doors designed for people dressed in conventional clothes. How should they exit? How high? In what position? There were a multitude of difficulties as well as exciting possibilities, and the nations of Europe were intent on developing the technique and making it a practical war winner for the next round.

One of the major problems jumpers faced was how to carry weapons. Their conclusion was that weapons shouldn't go with the trooper but should be stowed in containers that dropped at the same time as the jumpers. There were problems with this system, but it was retained (with variations) by all the combatants throughout the war that

Members of the 501st Parachute Infantry Battalion—the first US Army organization of tactical parachutists—head for the planes. Lawson Field, Fort Benning, April 1941.

followed. The Germans used metal carts, with little wheels and a handle, to drop rifles, radios, and the other tools and supplies of the trade. On landing, the jumpers ran around to collect their gear, which was sometimes nearby, sometimes in the next county. The design of the cart made it handy for moving loads — if the ground was hard.

During this time the United States was carefully avoiding the European war of words, and in the grand old tradition, tried to be buddies with everybody. The Depression was still in full swing, and the nation was in no mood to pump tax money into organizations like the army and the navy. The resources of the American army in 1939 were basically the resources and technologies left over from the First World War. Professional soldiers were paying close attention to the work of the Europeans, imagining ways of incorporating those developments into American tactics and strategy and planning for the future, but they were observers and not participants. Their time would come.

It would not be until 1939 that the United States Congress would authorize a modernization of its armed forces. The War Department G3 Section asked the chief of infantry to consider the possibility of something it called "air infantry," and to think about it quickly. The chief of infantry responded five days later with a report that described the future.

On 1 September of that year Germany attacked Poland using a combination of air and ground force; they promptly defeated the Polish army, which surrendered on the 27th. France and England declared war but did nothing.

On 30 November the USSR attacked Finland with a thirty-division assault along their entire border; small detachments of paratroopers were used, the first recorded application of airborne operations. The Finns stopped the Russians cold for a while.

In February 1940 the Infantry Board began work on the airborne infantry idea. They recommended development of a new kind of parachute for airborne operations and jump altitudes of between 300 and 500 feet.

In May Germany attacked Holland and Belgium, successfully using airborne and air assault techniques.

The United States now began investigating with enthusiasm the possibilities of airborne operations — only about ten years late. The Air Corps Test Center not only developed the T4 parachute that the Infantry Board had asked for, they threw in a novel concept — the reserve parachute. No other nation provided a reserve for its paratroopers during the war. The T4 had risers that permitted a jumper to control his descent more than with any other parachute — an important development. A platoon of volunteers was formed to test the concepts and techniques at a practical level, and the traditions of the contemporary airborne quickly developed, concentrating on intensive physical conditioning and instruction. The volunteers made their first jump on 16 August 1940 and soon made a highly favorable impression on the planners. The 501st Parachute Battalion was formed shortly thereafter, and in April 1941 a jump school was established at Fort Benning.

The 82nd Infantry Division had been deactivated after the Great War; now its colors were revived. While the division was training, it was decided to convert it to an airborne division, and to siphon off a cadre to form another airborne division, the 101st.

Training for water landings with an early version of the swing landing trainer at Fort Benning. The water was and still is made of sawdust.

While the United States Army was trying to adapt to the idea of an airborne, the Germans were about to reach the zenith of their operations with the invasion of British-held Crete. Although the invasion was successful, the cost was spectacularly high: 44 percent, including 3,000 killed, 8,000 wounded, 170 aircraft out of 530 lost. But only the Germans knew how bad the casualties were; the Allies were convinced that the airborne was an effective and efficient system, and they were ready to put it to work.

Both the 82nd and 101st Airborne Divisions were activated on 15 August 1942. They continued to prepare for combat, and on 9 July 1943, elements of the 82nd jumped into Sicily in one of

Troops load onto C-47s at dear old Fort Bragg, 1943, for an early air assault.

the most ill-organized and disastrous assaults by Allied units during the war. Numerous casualties were inflicted by friendly naval gunfire, which shot down many jump airplanes on their way to the assault. The drop zones were missed by many miles, and some jumpers were put out thirty miles from their objectives; some were dropped over the water. The enemy was defeated, but at a high cost in paratroopers. Even so, important lessons were learned, and many things worked correctly. The regiments were organized into "combat teams," with engineers, signal companies, and artillery.

During the remainder of the war, the airborne

refined and expanded its tools and techniques. Three other divisions were formed—the 11th, the 17th, and the 13th. The exploits and successes of these units are far too rich and varied to attempt to describe here in much detail, so they will only be summarized in the most superficial fashion. For a good historical overview, see Clay Blair's *Ridgway's Paratroopers* and Gerard Devin's *Paratrooper!*

The 82nd and 101st Divisions led the charge into Europe on 6 June 1944, but had many of the same difficulties they experienced on Sicily, with missed drop zones and strayed equipment. The forces were spread thinly and some found themselves quite alone on a darkened and hostile battlefield. Maxwell Taylor, the commander of 14,000 men, became the first American general to jump into combat. He was all by himself on the ground until he finally located one of his riflemen, who was also feeling quite lonely. They embraced and went off in search of companionship.

Although the drop was less organized on the ground than planned, it was successful in disrupting the Germans and slowing their reaction to the amphibious landings. The dispersion of the American units worked partly in favor of the attackers, confusing the enemy and giving the impression that there were more invaders than actually existed. Despite the cost in blood, 6 June was a lucky day for the invaders, because the Germans hesitated, and in hesitating, lost. To the airborne goes much of the honor for that pause.

There would be other jumps during the war, and the players gradually figured out the best ways to accomplish the numerous and critical jobs involved. By the time the 82nd made its fourth jump, into Holland, whole units actually were deposited right where they were supposed to be,

and in this case it was well behind enemy lines. They achieved complete surprise in a well planned and executed operation.

An important aspect of this period, which has never gotten sufficient attention, is the role of gliders in airborne operations. In fact, air mobility and air assault techniques were developed with a mix of equal parts glider and parachute forces. The glider riders took tremendous risks, in the air and on the ground, fully equal to those of the jumpers, but with less glory. The jumpers and the riders ended up on the same ground at about the same time, and fought the same enemy together. But the jumpers got jump pay and jump boots and media attention, while the glider riders got shot at. The flimsy aircraft were flown by pilots with little experience and training, who had to land where they could. Many crashed with the deaths of all aboard.

Many of the airborne-qualified troopers were used as conventional infantry because of the requirements of the moment and a lack of suitable missions. One of these units, the 11th Airborne, spent most of its life swatting Japanese and mosquitoes in the jungles of the South Pacific. Toward the end of the war, though, information was received that suggested the Japanese were about to slaughter a large number of prisoners held in a camp at Los Baños in the Philippines. The intel report indicated the executions would be in only a few days. An airborne assault on the camp was quickly planned, and the Los Baños raid has gone down in history as one of the most elegant and effective uses of airborne techniques. The prisoners were all freed moments before they were to be killed, just like in the movies.

Elements of the 101st and the 82nd were involved in the Battle of the Bulge, where their character contributed largely to the successful defense of the perimeter. The 82nd still maintains the legend of the rifleman who confronted an American tank crew retreating past him at some black moment during the German onslaught. The rifleman asked the tank crew if they were looking for a safe place to hide; they were. "PULL YOUR VEHICLE IN BEHIND ME," he yelled up at the tankers. "I'M THE 82ND AIRBORNE, AND THIS IS AS FAR AS THE BASTARDS ARE GOING!"

Three Medals of Honor were won by members of the 82nd during the war, along with 79 Dis-tinguished Service Crosses, 894 Silver Stars, and 2,478 Bronze Stars. In 442 days spent in combat, they lost 3,000 killed in action and 12,604 wounded in action.

The colors of the 82nd and the 11th were pre-served after the war, while the 101st, 13th, and 17th stood down. They've been used from time to time when professional soldiers were needed for an insurrection, a revolution, or a counterin-

77mm pack howitzer is loaded aport a Waco. Gliders played an unsung role in the early years of the airborne, delivering troops, vehicles and supplies to the DZ.

surgency. The airborne has been the faithful palace guard, the dependable and resourceful rapid reaction force from inception to the present day. In the case of the 82nd, this has meant trips to the Dominican Republic, Washington, D.C., Miami, Viet Nam, and many, many alerts.

The most recent serious use of airborne assault (at this writing) was Urgent Fury, the Grenada operation that began on 25 October 1983. Two 82nd Airborne Division brigade task forces were airlanded at Point Salines after Rangers were dropped onto the field to secure it. Although the jumpers were mostly from the Ranger battalions at Fort Benning, two of them came from the 82nd, and for one it was his "cherry" jump—the first after jump school. It got him and all the others who made the combat jump a small bronze star on their jump wings.

United States Army Combat Jumps

8 November 1942	509th PIR	Algeria
15 November 1942	509th PIR	Tunisia
9 July 1943	504th PIR	Sicily
5 September 1943	503rd PIR	Markham Valley
9 September 1943	504th PIR	Salerno
14 September 1943	509th PIR	Avellion
6 June 1944	101st Airborne Division	Normandy
6 June 1944	82nd Airborne Division	Normandy
3 July 1944	503rd PIR	Noemfoor Island
15 August 1944	1st Airborne Task Force	France
17 September 1944	101st Airborne Division	Nijmegen-Arnhem
17 September 1944	82nd Airborne Division	Nijmegen-Arnhem
3 February 1945	11th Airborne Division	Luzon
16 February 1945	503rd PIR	Corregidor
23 February 1945	11th Airborne Division	Los Baños
24 March 1945	17th Airborne Division	Germany
20 October 1950	187th ARCT	Korea
20 October 1950	187th ARCT	Korea
23 March 1951	187th ARCT	Korea
22 February 1967	173rd Airborne Brigade	Viet Nam
25 October 1983	1st and 2nd Battalions, 75th Rangers	Grenada

PIR: Parachute Infantry Regiment
ARCT: Airborne Regimental Combat Team

Blood Wings

So, you want to be airborne qualified? No problem! Anybody in the army can volunteer! It takes only three weeks; you spend lots of time in the fresh air and sunshine of scenic central Georgia, and a large staff of highly trained, attentive professionals will spare no effort to make your experience in the airborne course unforgettable in every way. You'll learn a number of aerobic exercise routines, memorize some amusing songs to sing on your daily outings, and romp on some fun playground apparatus. You'll come out in terrific physical condition. People pay hundreds of dollars a day to go to exclusive spas where they get back in shape and have a good time; but when you go to jump school, the army pays you! Not only that, you will learn all sorts of new skills and come out with a whole new outlook on life; you'll learn to pay attention, to respond instantly to commands, and enter that select group of people who know how to jump from airplanes. What a deal! Sign right here.

The airborne course at Fort Benning has become a national institution of higher learning, like Harvard or West Point in some ways but different in others. It works its magic in a hurry but leaves its impression on its graduates forever. It is a democratic place, accepting anybody who can meet the basic conditions for admission, including officers and privates; women and men; young and old; members of the marines, navy, air force, and coast guard. There are students from allied nations. There are seventeen-year-old ROTC students and forty-five-year-old colonels. They are all treated the same way, and that way is demanding.

They come for many reasons, some practical, others romantic. It is a ticket-punch for many officers, who have no interest in airborne ops but want to demonstrate the proper warrior spirit. For Special Forces aspirants, it is a requirement for admission to the club. For some it is simply a dream, a personal and professional goal to complete the course and be able to wear the wings. About one person in five in the whole army wears wings.

Every year 22,000 people graduate and about 2,200 don't. They arrive in taxis, buses, personal vehicles; in cowboy hats; in dress greens, blues, and whites. They form up around one of the NCOs from the reception center and clutch their orders, waiting for their names to be called. They are a rabble at this point, individuals in search of an identity. They stand around, wary and uneasy, uncertain what to do next. They will find out shortly.

"ANDERSON, MICHAEL T.," booms the sergeant. A navy ROTC cadet in gleaming whites steps out of line and approaches the NCO. He is eyed sharply by the sergeant: "It is perfectly all right with me *if you move a little faster!*" And that is exactly what he and all the other students start doing right away. They will be doing push-ups before they are through here. And they will be doing thousands of them before they graduate.

The mission of the school is straightforward and hasn't changed a lot in forty years. It is to qualify people to make military parachute jumps. Jumping from airplanes isn't a particularly big deal, and many civilians consider it a sport. Military jumping is a different game from sport jump-

Previous pages: Roster Number Two Two Zero executes an acceptable C-130 exit from the thirty-four-foot tower during the second week of the Basic Airborne Course. The next jumper begins to assume a good door position.

ing, however; it is a profession and a mind-set. Sport jumping is relatively safe and is supposed to be done for fun; military jumping is, by design, enmeshed in peril. It is a means to deliver people to battlefields to fight, to kill and be killed. It isn't supposed to be fun, although when green tracers light your way, it can be rather thrilling.

Military jumps are made from low altitudes, with crowds of people in each other's way, thrashing quickly to the ground, encumbered by weapons and equipment. If something goes wrong (and it does), a jumper has eight seconds to fix it before making a mess on the DZ. Eight seconds is from normal jump altitude; in combat it is less. When the airborne soldiers get to the ground, their work begins; they must be effective or they will be a handicap to the others. It is the duty of the staff of the school to ensure that the men and women who graduate really have earned the jump wings they are allowed to wear. The staff has done its job so

Sergeant Knox welcomes the new students as they report in to the Basic Airborne Course. The attire is soon replaced by BDUs, and the casual posture will be replaced with the Position of Attention or the Front Leaning Rest.

"Son, you are suffering from vapor lock of the cranial cavity, and that is a *leg* disease!" Lieutenant Colonel Scott, Airborne Ranger, commander of the school, counsels a student about his progress.

well over the decades that jump wings remain one of the most universally respected decorations on the uniforms of those who serve in the American military. Nobody, not senior officers or NCOs or pretty females, gets through jump school without a lot of hard work and a lot of very prompt reactions to instructions. This is one place in the army where rank does not have its privileges.

To attend, a male student must be able to do forty-five *correct* push-ups in two minutes, forty-five *correct* sit-ups in two minutes, and run two miles in less than sixteen minutes. Women have a different set of requirements; their mile is slower, their pull-ups are done with feet on the ground from an inclined position. Women students have less stringent requirements because of army regulations, but other than that, they are cut no slack and their minimums are not exactly easy. The

36

minimums are just to *get in*. Once in, the students have to improve, and those who don't do well enough recycle until they do, or they quit. Physical training includes a warm-up, a run, a cooldown, and then pull-ups. Those are followed by high jumpers, push-ups, sit-ups, trunk twisters, body twisters, and knee bends. The exercises consume at least an hour of the day. For those whose performance during formation and inspection was found deficient, there is a special area for PT, where it is even more intense and exhausting than the normal routine. It isn't supposed to be harassment or abuse, but it is very, very hard, and whatever you did to get here is something you will not intentionally repeat.

The staff are intolerant of anything that looks complacent or careless, and they look hard for those dangerous qualities. During inspection in the morning they look carefully at haircuts, shaves, boots, and uniforms. The era of heavy

Neither size nor gender prevent people from attending the school, and women sometimes excel in what was once a strictly man's school. Many women graduates go on to become riggers.

37

starch and spit-shined boots is gone, replaced by "fluff and buff," but uniforms must be well fluffed, buttons buttoned, and boots perfectly buffed. Deficiencies are costly. Two major gigs of the same type can get you recycled. Three can get you out of the school and back to your unit. It's easy to get gigged. The Black Hats are looking for any lack of motivation, and they jump, quickly and hard, on anybody they think is suspect. To tolerate all this you really have to *want* to be here.

About one in ten will fail. Four in a hundred quit at some point in the course. Another four have medical problems that can't be resolved within thirty days. One and a half percent are removed for administrative reasons, such as disciplinary or personal problems, and one person in two hundred will fail to keep up on PT runs or will not qualify on one of the apparatus.

The school has a reputation for demanding a kind of formal military behavior and obedience that is found within the entire army community only here, at West Point, and a few other places. There is a tremendous sense of ritual and tradition. Everything a student does is done formally. Language is formal; posture is formal. In the rest of the army, a captain or a major expects the enlisted folks to hop and pop, to snap to attention or to defer with a respectful "yes, sir!" At the airborne course, those officers had better be prepared to have the tables turned. That's part of the game; when the Black Hat says "drop!" you'd better get down and knock them out, and jump up with a mighty "AIRBORNE!" when you're done, captain, or it's down for more. It's all for a reason: you've got to train yourself to react correctly and instinctively when you start jumping from airplanes on military missions. You have to do the right thing, right now, or you could kill yourself, or — worse still — endanger your unit's military mission.

GROUND WEEK

There is a ritual to the whole experience. First, inspection, then physical training. PT is a very important part of the school. It helps prevent injuries, improves control and coordination, and separates those who really want to be here from those whose commitment is weaker. It is really not that strenuous, and some of the people find it rather easy. Compared to the demands of Ranger school, for instance, it is tame stuff. But for the majority of the people who attend, it provides enough challenge. The PT part of instruction begins with a run on a mile-long track around the school. The week begins with just two orbits at a pace that starts rather slowly and then accelerates. The distance increases during the week, with Friday being the big day — a four-mile run. Students fall out of formation and struggle along.

The first day, many of the students are in a daze, and a lot of them are not prepared for inspection. Some of them quit — a few even before the first day begins. The second day, more are gone and some are still trying to catch on. By the third day, most are getting into the routine — they "snap and pop" the way they're supposed to. Students are addressed by the large number on their helmets, or simply as "airborne." The accepted

Left: Welcome to the Gig Pit! This is where you go to think about the way you buffed your boots this morning. The "front leaning rest" position is one of the instructional tools used by the staff to encourage people to pay attention to detail.

response to almost any comment or instruction is a loud "CLEAR, SERGEANT! AIRBORNE!"

The instruction is fast and furious and includes the five points of performance nomenclature, the proper way to respond to the jumpmaster's commands inside the aircraft, fitting the harness, and how to execute a parachute landing fall (PLF). There is practice at the mock door at ground level and with the wind machine.

The mock door suggests the basic contours of a cargo aircraft; it is here that the students begin to feel that there are other things to do besides push-ups. They put on parachutes for the first time, even though they are just dummy training assemblies, and become used to the feel of the harness and the weight of the main and reserve. They learn to shuffle inside the aircraft, how to stand in the door, the proper exit technique (jump up and out for a C-130, walk out for a C-141), and how to count from one to four. While these skills seem simple and elementary, it is amazing how people can screw them up, but a few hundred push-ups and a kind word or two from the attending Black Hat is usually all it takes to correct a student.

Then, the exercise is expanded to include the routine of canopy checking and reserve deployment. This simple drill is practiced over and over and over — for a reason: in the aircraft, or falling through the air, nobody has the luxury of time to think about what to do, particularly when something goes wrong. It is automatic, or it is too late.

TOWER WEEK

By the time the second week has begun, the students have come out of their daze; many are beginning to enjoy the process of instruction, and even some of the instructors. The second week is Tower Week, and now things start to get interesting.

There are several areas on the grounds of the school where instruments of torture are arranged. One of these is a collection of towers with cabin mock-ups thirty-four feet off the ground. There are swing landing trainers and a lateral drift apparatus.

The morning run on the one-mile track is still difficult for some, but there is pleasure in running in step and singing the "jody calls." The Black Hat sings the line, the troops sing it back at him:

> Airborne Ranger, raving mad,
> he's got a patch I wish I had.
> Yellow and black and halfmoon shape,
> Airborne Ranger — he's gone ape!

The high point of the week, in every respect, is the thirty-four-foot tower, which starts putting a lot of skills to use. The tower is high enough to scare some students; for a few it is worse than jumping from the aircraft during the following week. There are doors on both sides of the cabin mock-up, with four cables running past them. Each cable has a trolley on it, with a riser that is attachable to the harness each student wears. It is a primary training apparatus, and each student will spend a lot of time in and around it. The training progresses in two parts: the first is essentially the same as on the mock door, but well off the ground; the advanced phase develops skills for

Right: Charlie One One Three assumes the Letup Position in the suspended harness, where you learn turns, slips, maneuvers with the T10 and MC1-1B, landing attitude, and emergency landings.

Now, this is fun! The tower is where it starts to feel like you're getting serious. It's only 34 feet, but that's enough to scare some people.

mass tactical exit techniques and for dealing with malfunctions. When you stand in the door of the cabin mock-up during the first week, the drop is only about eighteen inches to the ground, and the only thing to fear is the wrath of the attending Black Hat. Now, you know there is something physically threatening. During the climb up the stairs the first time, anxieties develop. It starts to look and feel a little dangerous, and when you arrive at the top, the entire tower vibrates enough to get your attention. The tower is built from

wooden telephone poles, and it wobbles as people move around on it. (If you and a few others work together, you can really annoy the instructors by using your body weight to wiggle the tower back and forth—until they scream at you to cut it out.) By the door is an instructor who is all business, and expects you to be, too. Below, in a little throne room, sits a Black Hat with his clipboard, waiting to grade every student on each point of performance.

The Black Hat looks for common errors: weak exit (falling or diving out, shoving with the hands) instead of the proper strong hop up and out; jumpers with their head up or knees bent or feet apart; jumpers who grab for the risers as soon as they leave the door or who put their hands on top of the reserve or wrap their arms around it; jumpers who close their eyes or count too fast or too slow or not at all. At first, the students work on these techniques as individuals. But combat jumps require a stick of jumpers to exit at one-second intervals, to keep people together on the ground while providing separation in the air. And it is a lot harder to assume a good door position or body position when you're following a gaggle of people all at once, each laden with a rucksack and weapons container. So that gets practiced, too, over and over.

"One One Four, first jumper, sergeant! AIRBORNE!" announces a captain as he snaps and pops in front of the staff sergeant who will critique him.

"Satisfactory," is all the praise he gets. "Now, get up there and do a C-141 exit."

"CLEAR, SERGEANT! AIRBORNE!"

"One sixteen, sergeant! AIRBORNE!" announces the next jumper. He stands there and the Black Hat just looks at him—waiting. Then he remembers, and adds, "Second jumper!"

"You didn't have your hands on the outside of the aircraft."

"CLEAR, SERGEANT! AIRBORNE!"

"That's the third time in a row you've done that now. You might not even qualify."

"CLEAR, SERGEANT! AIRBORNE!" and he's off to try it again. And so it goes.

The level of enthusiasm rises during the second week as people become accustomed to the demanding routine and begin to feel that success is attainable. The Black Hats' lectures draw a particular kind of reaction that is a combination of agreement and applause—the "Ranger bark." During demonstrations and PT, when a Black Hat demands "IS THAT CLEAR, AIRBORNE?" he will get a lot of cheerful growls and "ARFs!" mixed in with the "CLEAR, SERGEANT! AIRBORNE!!"

JUMP WEEK

Ground Week is over. Tower Week is over. Jump Week has arrived. It begins early on Monday morning with the usual routine, then it's off to

CLEAR THE PLATFORM! The swing landing trainer is used to learn what happens during the last fractions of a second before you do your PLF (parachute landing fall).

the rigging sheds down by Lawson Field. It takes a while to rig and check 500 students. They draw their parachutes, team up with a buddy, and begin the careful process of adjusting and donning the equipment. People come in all sizes, but the T10s in only four, so straps have to be adjusted and arranged. The teams assist and inspect each other as they go along.

Then the jumpmaster and his assistants begin the inspections. Each jumper presents himself in turn and dozens of points are carefully checked: helmet, for absence of sharp edges, correct neck-strap fitting, liner pad installed; canopy releases and riser assemblies; chest straps; quick-release assemblies, back straps, and waistband, all for proper assembly and fit and condition. The reserve is checked for secure connectors; safety wire installed; grip handle in correct position; stow pocket clear; pins straight, clean, correctly routed; pack opening bands in good shape, correctly attached. The static line is routed to the proper side (depending on which door the jumper will use) and correctly stowed; the snaphook is checked to see if it's in good condition, functions correctly, and has the safety wire and lanyard attached. With his fingers the jumpmaster traces the static line over the shoulder to verify that it isn't frayed, broken, cut, or misrouted. Later, for the combat jumps, rucksacks and weapons are added to the list of things to be checked. Each jumper is carefully inspected, approved, then sent off to wait for the next act of the drama, the briefing.

Left: The jumpmaster performs his safety check, observing the DZ and the airspace below for unsafe conditions, before commanding STAND IN THE DOOR! *Right:* PREPARE TO LAND! Risers to chest, elbows against body, head up, legs straight, knees unlocked, feet and knees together.

Left to right: GET READY! Directs attention to the Jump-master. CHECK STATIC LINES! Snaphook correctly attached to cable, safety wire installed, static line in good shape, no slack, pack closing tie correct. CHECK EQUIPMENT! Everything safe and correct. STAND IN THE DOOR! Assume a good door position, await the command to GO.

The jumpers file into an auditorium used only for such briefings, with benches designed for people whose clothing is a little bulkier than normal. It is dim in the building, but outside in the bright sunlight can be seen the waiting Hercules. The stage is a platform with a podium, and the set is a large lighted map of Fryar drop zone, across the river, just a hop, skip, and a jump away from Lawson Field.

A chaplain comes in, introduces himself, and leads the jumpers in a prayer. Then a Black Hat steps forward and leads the multitude in song; for decades they've been singing "Blood Upon the Risers":

> He was just a rookie trooper
> and he surely shook with fright.
> Checked all his equipment
> and made sure his pack was tight.

He had to sit and listen
to the awful engines roar,
And he ain't gonna jump no more!

> Gory, gory, what a hell of a way to die,
> Gory, gory, what a hell of a way to die,
> Gory, gory, what a hell of a way to die,
> And he ain't gonna jump no more!

It goes on forever in a multitude of verses designed to reassure absolutely nobody, but it helps break some of the tension—or, for some, to build it. Outside, the two C-130s wait, ramps down.

The Black Hat begins the briefing using the map on the wall behind him: "Good news, Airborne: there is no wind on the drop zone, no wind!"

They respond as a chorus, first with cheers, then they chant: "FIRED UP! FIRED UP! FIRED UP! FIRED UP!"

This is the last time to put it all together, and the Black Hat summarizes two weeks of instruction before sending the jumpers out to the aircraft.

"All right, Airborne, direct your attention to the side of the board! JUMP AIRCRAFT: C-130. JUMP ALTITUDE: TWELVE HUNDRED AND FIFTY FEET. Now, remember what I told you. No running inside the aircraft! Shuffle to the door! Once you get to the door, hand your static line to the jumpmaster. Once he takes it, you let go! Your hand goes down! First man in the door, assume a good door position, back straight, hands on the outside of the door. When the jumpmaster taps you on the buttocks, you exit the aircraft! Is that clear?"

"CLEAR, SERGEANT! AIRBORNE!!"

"Once you get out of the aircraft, check body position and count! At the end of the four thousand count, you should feel the opening shock; if you do not feel the opening shock, remain in a tight body position and activate your reserve parachute.

"Everybody will be jumping the T10 parachute. There should be no holes in the T10 parachute except at the very top, at the apex! IF YOU SEE ANY OTHER HOLES, DON'T GO ACTIVATING YOUR RESERVE JUST YET!

MONITOR THE HOLES! Look around and see if you are falling faster than the other jumpers; if you are falling faster than the other jumpers, assume a good tight body position and activate your reserve.

"If you have a good canopy, keep a sharp lookout during descent. Look all around you, at the other jumpers in the air. If you get too close to somebody, slip away. Now, if you look up and find yourself with a face full of suspension lines, get in a spread eagle position and try to bounce off the suspension lines. Is that clear?"

"CLEAR, SERGEANT! AIRBORNE!"

"Right. When you are about 200 feet above the ground, locate the smoke on the south end or the north end of the drop zone. Look at the smoke and determine your direction of drift. At about a hundred feet above the ground, once you have determined your direction of drift, go ahead and reach up there and pull a riser down in the opposite direction of drift. Get your feet and knees together and relax. Assume a good prepare-to-land attitude. Once the balls of the feet strike the ground, execute a good parachute landing fall

MAINTAIN A GOOD BODY POSITION AND COUNT!
Jumpers exit a C-130 at one-second intervals.

utilizing the five points of contact. What are the five points of contact?"

"BALLS OF FEET! CALF! THIGH! BUTTOCKS! SIDE MUSCLES OF THE BACK!"

"Any questions? Everybody ready to go?"

"FIRED UP! FIRED UP! FIRED UP! FIRED UP!"

"EVERYBODY ON THEIR FEET!"

Five hundred voices roar: "AIRBORNE!"

The students will make five jumps, normally one each day. The first is a "Hollywood" jump, a daylight jump without combat equipment. They'll make three jumps with the T10, two with the steerable MC1-1B. One of the T10 jumps will be at night.

They file aboard in their sticks, filling the cavernous Hercules. It is awkward to waddle around wearing the two parachutes. The troops seats are designed to accommodate jumpers with parachutes, and each seat belt could accommodate someone with a sixty-inch waistline. Significant looks are exchanged: here we go! The engines start with the rising whine of turbines, and the special perfume of JP5 exhaust fills the air. Brakes released, throttles forward, the bird pushes off down the runway of the same airfield where the first American jumpers went aloft four and a half decades before.

The C-130 is a wonderful aircraft, the functional heir to the fabled C-47. From the flight deck you have the feeling of flying behind a huge picture window in bright sunshine, the four big turboprops making their powerful music somewhere astern. The earth glides smoothly below in a purposeful way. But back in the cargo compartment it is dark, noisy, and crowded. Conversation is almost impossible, and any sense of what is going on outside is ascertained mainly by imagining. Overhead the cables and push rods and ductwork of the bird are exposed for the amusement of the inmates. The aircrew gleefully condemns the mental capacity of anybody who would jump from a perfectly good airplane; the jumpers respond that there is no such thing as a perfectly good airplane.

Too soon, it seems, the plane is level. Until now the operation is all air force, with the army people guests, along for the ride. It is a potentially awkward situation; who is in control? The standard operating procedure is that the aircrew is in charge right up to the moment when the door is ready to be opened. Then, the responsibility for what happens at the door shifts to the jumpmaster. The aircraft commander tells the loadmaster in the cabin, "Three minutes." The loadmaster turns to the jumpmaster and yells over the noise, "IT'S YOUR DOOR, ARMY!" He releases the lock and the big door slides up and locks overhead, adding light and noise to the interior. Below, the trees and contours of rural Alabama slide past relentlessly. Six minutes out, the aircraft commander notifies the jumpmaster; the sequence of commands begins.

The jumpmaster hooks up, looks at the stick of jumpers, and commands, "GET READY!"

You lean forward, poised, hands on knees, one foot under the seat and one in the aisle—ready. Three minutes out, the doors open, air deflectors are deployed, jump platforms are extended and locked. The pilot throttles back and slows down the aircraft to jump speed.

The jumpmaster does a 360-degree air safety check, pops back in, and commands, "OUTBOARD PERSONNEL, STAND UP!" It is too crowded for us all to get up at once, so the outboard jumpers get up and secure the seats.

"INBOARD PERSONNEL, STAND UP!" Now we are all up, the seats released and secured. Turn toward the jumpmaster, watch, wait. The jumpmaster commands, "HOOK UP!"

Unsnap the hook from the reserve carrying handle, reach up and clip it to the anchor line; slip the safety wire into the hole, toward the aft end of the aircraft, and bend it down. Take the slack out of the static line by forming a bight at eye level and hold it. Turn toward the jumpmaster, watch, wait. He commands, "CHECK STATIC LINES!"

Last chance to check it out; look at it and feel it from your shoulder up to the anchor line; check it for frays or tears, proper attachment, proper routing, no excessive slack. Turn toward the jumpmaster, watch, wait. He commands, "CHECK EQUIPMENT!"

With one hand still on the static line, use the other hand to quickly frisk yourself for any unsafe

A C-5A stands by at Green Ramp to receive army equipment for deployment on Operation Market Time.

Second Point of Performance: Check canopy and gain control.

conditions. You're good to go. Turn toward the jumpmaster, watch, wait. He commands, "SOUND OFF FOR EQUIPMENT CHECK!"

The last man in the stick sounds off, "OKAY!" and taps the jumper in front of him, who repeats the signal until it gets to you. "OKAY!" you yell, and pass it along. The stick leader looks the jumpmaster in the eye and declares, "ALL OKAY!"

The jumpmaster performs a little routine now, and the students watch in fascination. He slams one foot on the right side of the open door, then on the left, verifying that the platform is secured and locked. Gripping each side of the door, he leans out, projecting himself into the blast outside for a better view. He is performing a last safety check, verifying the location of the DZ, an absence of nearby airplanes or water, or red smoke on the ground. Then, with a gesture to the stick leader, he commands, "STAND IN THE DOOR!"

For the first jump, each student is tapped out individually, one at a time. The stick leader is there one heartbeat, the next he's gone. The second student hears the command, "STAND IN THE DOOR!", assumes the proper position, gets swatted, and is gone. Now there isn't anyone else between you and the jumpmaster. "STAND IN THE DOOR!" Just like in ground week, there you stand, coiled, hands on the outside of the aircraft, eyes on the horizon, but unlike ground week, the ground moves below you. Stand there, watch the horizon, wait. . . .

"GO!"

What is it like to actually jump, to make the step into space? For two weeks you've been working toward this moment, and now it all comes together. For some, it is just a blur, and they don't really remember to count. For others, it is painless and elegant, a performance to be proud of. For most, it is somewhere in between.

The First Point of Performance: a good body position and count.

The muscles you've been building spring you up and out into the blast. By reflex, you count, loud enough for them to hear on the ground below: "ONE THOUSAND, TWO THOUSAND, THREE THOUSAND, FOUR THOUSAND. . . ."

You keep your eyes open, chin down on chest, elbows in against your sides, fingers spread and clutching the sides of the reserve, your right hand covering the reserve ripcord. You lock your legs together and keep your knees straight, toes down. Your body is bent forward and you can inspect the shine on your boot toes: it's still pretty good. The canopy opens with a rustle, the sound and fury of the aircraft are suddenly gone, and you begin the damnedest ride anybody ever had.

The Second Point of Performance: check canopy and immediately gain control.

You know it when the canopy opens. It isn't uncomfortable and it doesn't hurt—you just aren't falling anymore. The sound of the opening is also a pleasure, a kind of rustling followed by a soft little pop as the great thirty-five-foot sail bites the air. The suspension lines frequently will twist a bit during the deployment, and it takes a few seconds and some kicking maneuvers to straighten things out.

The noise of the aircraft fades from full blast to gentle purr. You lean back and take a good look at the lovely canopy, pulsing in the air as though it were alive. The harness is comfortable now. You are sort of sitting within its confines, and the feeling is quite secure. It is disconcerting to see your feet with not a damn thing beneath them but a thousand feet of air. You are drifting above and below and alongside other jumpers.

From the ground, a Black Hat uses a huge public address system to admonish the jumpers: CHECK CANOPY! CHECK CANOPY! He will throw in tidbits of advice as required. Even in the

A stick leader prepares for his first jump. The jumpmaster is still completing his safety check.

Here's the hardcore way to wear your wings — pinned directly to your body with a friendly little tap from your beloved student company commander. This is by request only.

air the jumpers are not safe from the watchful eyes of their instructors.

The Third Point of Performance: keep a sharp lookout during descent.

There are a lot of people in the air during the mass tactical jumps, when jumpers exit at one-second intervals. It is easy to crash into somebody else, or into his canopy or suspension lines. Occasionally, a jumper will swing into and under another jumper's canopy, creating a lot of consternation and confusion but not a high degree of hazard. Sometimes one jumper will find himself walking on the top of another's canopy, in which case he needs to walk off promptly.

The Fourth Point of Performance: prepare to land.

The ride does not last forever. The sense of floating above the earth soon changes to a sensation of the earth rising toward you with slowly gathering speed. The lower you get, the faster it seems. You turn into the wind; head up, look at the horizon; feet and knees pressed tightly together; elbows in against the body, and hands pulling firmly down on the front risers. You need to keep your leg muscles tensed but not locked. The ground moves toward you with relentless acceleration. On your first jump, you aren't very good at picking a landing spot, and maneuvering the T10 is an art form yet to be fully mastered.

The Fifth Point of Performance: land.

You're going to do a PLF one way or another, and you'll see plenty of variations out on the DZ. But if you get it right after all that practice, you'll convert your vertical motion to horizontal motion with a graceful roll along the side of the body that begins with the balls of the feet, progresses up the side of the leg to your rear, to your upper back muscles. You can't think about it, you simply have to do it, and being in the right position when you hit the ground will have a lot to do with how comfortable it feels. You see two-point landings — feet and rear end — that look as though they should cause paralysis; but the kids are flexible. You try not to land in the creek. The Black Hats will drop you for that, or if they see you land with your feet apart — if you don't break anything.

At last, Jump Week is over, the fifth jump done, and it's time to get your wings. The Black Hats, who seem at times so intent on criticism and discipline, soften a little today. They carry a few wings with them out on the drop zone, and if somebody is injured and can't make it back on his or her own, they get pinned right there in the weeds of Fryar DZ.

Back in the bleachers are the friends and family who've come to observe the great moment. Some are proud fathers who know about the airborne mystique; there are mothers and sisters and brothers who really don't know what the fuss is about. One elegant young lady doesn't really care; she is waiting for her trooper to get through with this silliness so they can get married. She seeks out the lieutenant colonel who is the commander of the school and demands as politely as she can, "What can you do to expedite things? We're supposed to be getting married in two hours!" He is tolerant, charming, and reassuring to her, an image the troops didn't see often during the course. And soon his company is formed up and the presentations begin.

The students stand at attention and receive their wings from favorite Black Hats or staff; some want theirs from the colonel, whom they like very much. Some ask for theirs from the company commander or a particular NCO. Many request "blood wings." Those get pinned to your *body,* not just your shirt!

When you forget to keep your feet and knees together, sometimes it hurts. When it's on your fifth jump, the Black Hats show up with a few wings in their pockets.

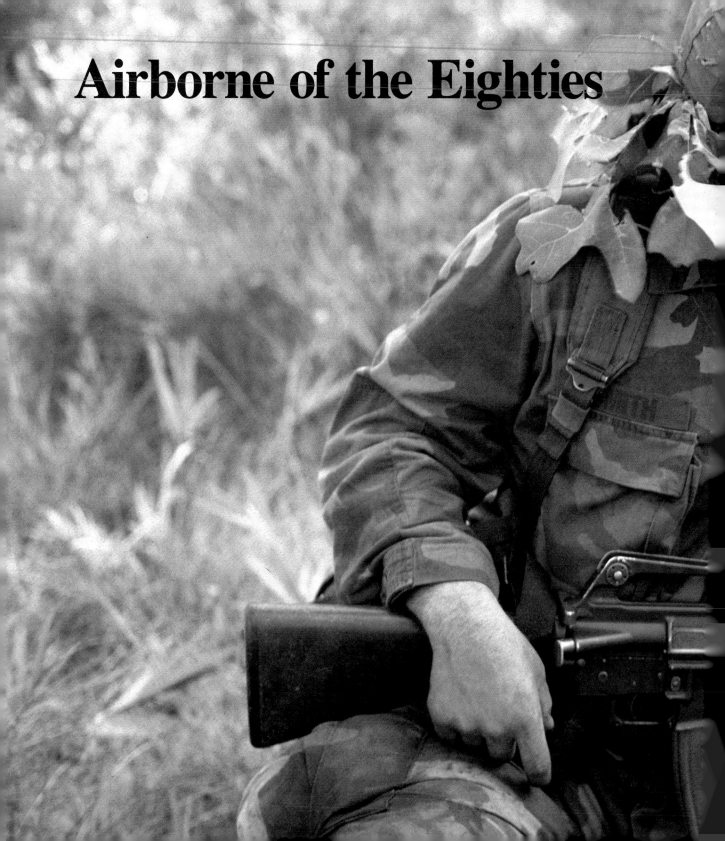

Airborne of the Eighties

Although this book is essentially about the conventional United States forces that rely on parachutes, there is more to the story than that. Other nations have airborne troops, and some have a lot more than we do.

The British, as in so many things, are our mentors and inspiration. We wear maroon berets because that is the British airborne color. British airborne training is far more demanding than ours, with a failure rate of 60 percent during the twenty-two-week course full of battle marches and assault courses. When someone completes their airborne course, they have survived a program that is like a combination of both our ranger and airborne schools. An English paratrooper would think our Basic Airborne Course incredibly easy, and by comparison it is. Their training is a big reason that the British prevailed in the Falklands, where 2nd and 3rd Parachute Regiments overwhelmed their opposition not so much with weapons but with style. They marched where they shouldn't have been able to march ("tabbing," they call it), attacked when the Argentines were too cold to even defend.

The Soviets have eight airborne divisions, each about half the size of our divisions but quite potent just the same. Each regiment has 164 officers and about 1,400 troops. The 76th Guards Red Banner Airborne Division is supposed to be the best of the lot, with a lineage that goes back sixty years to when it was born (like our 82nd) as an infantry unit. It earned a "Guards" title during the Battle of Stalingrad, and is now one of the reliable forces the Soviets depend on for power projection outside their borders.

There are some curious qualities to the way the Russians do business. The Soviet Union gets its soldiers entirely from conscription. But once drafted, men may volunteer for the airborne. Often these men have already been to jump school while civilians, as part of the DOSAAF program, somewhat like our high school ROTC. Divisions like the 76th Guards are unusual in that the troops are, like the jumpers of all other nations, a cut or two above the rest. Independence, imagination, and initiative are characteristics not usually found in most Soviet military organizations, but they are encouraged in the airborne units.

Another curiosity about the 76th Guards is that its makeup is rather restricted; ethnic minorities seem to have been prevented from joining. It is an almost completely Slavic unit, which seems to be manned almost entirely by members of the Communist party.

The Chinese also have an airborne, and an American general was recently allowed to jump with them. They do things a little differently, he reported. For one thing, they don't have canopy releases, so everybody carries a knife to cut away the canopy when the need arises. For another, they run with the wind when landing, and instead of doing a PLF, they hit the ground running — in order to catch and subdue the canopy.

The American airborne today lives several lives, most of them army, but there are airborne-qualified marines, navy, air force, and coast guard personnel and units that use them. Other than OSS drops into Europe during World War II, until Viet Nam, airborne meant strictly static line, mass tactical drops. Then, beginning in the early

Previous page: It must be the first day of the exercise, because our hero is still clean. His weapon is the M203 combination of rifle and grenade launcher. It will stay clean, but its owner won't.

58

1960s, the need evolved to sneak one or a few friendly folks into Indian country without being too obvious about it. One of the methods developed was the HALO jump, which stands for "high altitude (exit) low opening." The trick involved leaving an airplane far above the ground, freefalling to a minimum safe altitude, then deploying the parachute and landing before anybody noticed. It evolved into a standard technique for the unconventional forces to use, and there is a HALO school that teaches it. There are other techniques, like high altitude, high opening (HAHO), which involves an opening at high altitude and the ability to glide silently for miles through the night, to land silently in the middle of an enemy compound, say, without detection.

The Special Forces guys like to tell about a technique one of their members developed at HALO school a few years ago. They call it "The

A scout platoon climbs aboard a Chinook, the workhorse helicopter that first helped make airmobility a success way back in 1964, and is still doing well today.

Viper and the Jump from the Space Shuttle." The Viper, a senior NCO, was making his last qualification jump at the school, jumping from a ridiculously high altitude, with oxygen. After falling for a week or so, the Viper activated his main, which didn't work very well. "I wasn't really worried until I started going past the tops of the trees," he is alleged to have said later. His accomplices on the ground watched Viper burning in at the speed of heat, without a canopy, and ran to the spot with rakes and shovels to clean up the mess. But lo (and to say nothing of behold) up stood their hero, the inventor of the HANO (High Altitude, No Opening) technique. Those SF guys are not only tough, they're inventive!

THE AMERICAN AIRBORNE CONCEPT

The biggest, most obvious American airborne unit today is the 82nd Airborne Division, with about 15,000 people, almost all of whom are jumpers. The division represents the conventional force application of airborne and air assault techniques in the world of warfare. But there are a great many other applications and units that are staffed with people on jump status. There is the Special Forces (the fabled "Green Berets"); the navy's SEALs; the Rangers; and a wide variety of specialized operations, some clandestine, some not. Within the vast expanse of the 82nd's home port of Fort Bragg are many little compounds

Left: Specialist Fourth Class Hurlock, A Company, 2nd Battalion, 325th Airborne Infantry Regiment. The army rifleman is the ultimate weapon in the AirLand Battle. *Right:* Rapelling from a Blackhawk helicopter.

surrounded by tall fences and wire and guards, with high earth berms to prevent observation of the goings-on. Within these compounds is supposed to reside the DELTA force, the nation's most unconventional of unconventional warriors, about whom army public affairs is sworn to profess ignorance. Parachuting is one of the skills required of almost all of the people within the Special Operations Forces, and they've developed it to a fine art. They and the other unconventional warriors use a whole set of alternative techniques for getting to their objectives — free-fall parachuting techniques like HALO, HAHO, and, so they say, HANO.

The 82nd is the old, traditional, conventional division-sized unit with the T10s and MC1-1B static line parachutes and the mass tactical drops. The concept of the 82nd is to provide a large, extremely mobile force of division size that can go anywhere and fight on arrival. The marines used to have this function, and they do it well if you've got the time for their ships to get them to the scene of the crime. And, the objective needs damp edges — they are a rapid deployment force for maritime locations. The 82nd provides much the same function, but instead of a beach, they need a large, flat landing spot. Plus, they arrive at an indicated air speed of several hundred knots, which cuts down significantly on travel time.

The division is used as a kind of fire department, a unit that can move quickly to an emergency, bringing with it the tools and techniques to put out fires and restore order. The emergencies

that need military force in a hurry have come along with rather predictable regularity. Not the big, messy wars but the little incidents. There are enough people in the world who make up the rules as they go along that we need police forces, and that is one of the reasons we maintain a military. By maintaining it in a capable and visible way, tyrants are encouraged to think twice.

The 82nd is also used as one of the many infantry divisions the army maintains. It is a unit that can be committed to conventional battle with other divisions, although that would be a waste of many of its capabilities. The division can, as happened in Normandy, be placed within enemy territory to control terrain or gnaw on the opposition while waiting for other units to join it. The 82nd is, as infantry units go, a bit light in some resources (like large artillery), but it is heavy in others, and the whole effect is of a highly mobile force, offensive rather than defensive.

The 82nd has three basic tasks to plan for. The first is to be deployed by air; either jump or land on an objective; and find, fix, and destroy the enemy in a low- to mid-intensity conflict. The second is to jump or airland on objectives as part of a bigger force in a high-intensity conflict. The third is to execute small-scale unconventional missions. It can move by air to any location to scare the socks off a potential adversary.

The division, and most of the rest of the airborne, has to work closely with the air force. This isn't always easy for either of them, given the egos involved and the traditions of rivalry, but the 82nd and the folks right next door at Pope Air Force Base usually get along well. The air force provides the enormous C-141 and C-130 transport aircraft on which the division depends for delivery, as well as the fighters that cover and support

Left: In the horrendous downwash from a Chinook helicopter hovering above, a soldier strains to attach a trailer's sling to the cargo hook. It's a good idea to get off before the helicopter departs.

the assault. When it's time to go, there had better be a bunch of airframes lined up on the ramp, since even a company with a minimum of accessories requires four C-130s—three for the troops and one for the bulky cargo. The whole division requires 193 C-130 sorties just for the troops and 1,767 sorties for the cargo. The C-141 holds much more, but there are fewer of them available. Eighty-six C-141 sorties will deliver the jumpers of the division and 700 more will bring their equipment and supplies. So, the air force is part of the division in an essential way, in spite of all the rude remarks they make about people who jump from perfectly good airplanes.

The United States Air Force maintains a big, capable fleet of what they think are perfectly good airplanes that can carry the troops anywhere in the world their commander in chief wants them, without reservations. In fact, the air force doesn't maintain airplanes on call for the division but can pull in whatever is needed from whatever happens to be on the lot. About nine C-130s or five C-141s—enough aircraft to move a battalion (about 1,000 people in the Division Ready Force One)—can be sitting at the apron at Pope, ramp down, in ten hours. These planes can fly spectacular distances and stay aloft for what seems like an eternity (especially to the passengers), deploying troops with or without benefit of a staging base. Their crews are the paratroopers' friendly cousins-at-arms, with a whole different attitude toward the airborne. But they're here to help keep the army from turning things into a goatscrew. "World's highest paid, best educated trash haulers! You call, we haul! Anything, anytime, anyplace. Offering whisper-jet prop service to any hole in the world. NO load/runway/weather/move/cargo TOO heavy/short/bad/far/

sensitive." It says so on their business cards.

A staging base is some convenient spot where everybody stops for a bit to get their collective and individual acts together before going to work. A staging base is a handy spot to put on parachutes and do rigger checks. Helicopters are assembled here. Without a staging base, the troops chute up while in flight. The aircraft sent to Grenada carried parachutes for the troops to put on if the decision to jump was made; several hours into the flight the general in the lead aircraft decided to airland the force instead of airdrop, much to the men's disgust.

Although the division is called airborne and its disciples are all jumpers, they are not *always* delivered by parachute. When appropriate, the jumpers are put ashore from planes that land on the objective. The C-130 is tolerant of short dirt runways, and the 141 can land on an enemy's runway if it's long enough. That's how they did it in Grenada: the Rangers jumped onto the airfield and got the anti-invasion obstacles out of the way; then the C-141s came in and landed, one at a time, and delivered the goods right to the edge of the combat zone.

Like a fire department, the division is always on call, but not everyone is always on duty. The 15,000 people who wear the 82nd patch are nearly 100 percent parachute qualified. They are members of three infantry regiments, artillery battalions, support units, aviation and engineer

---

Right: A Blackhawk helicopter crew finishes the checklist before pulling pitch to participate in an exercise. They are part of the OPFOR and have embellished their beast with temporary insignia.

units, and all of the other organizations a division needs.

Societies such as the 82nd Airborne have traditionally been highly masculine enclaves, and still are to a degree. But, for a variety of reasons, women are being admitted to the club. There are about 220 females in the 82nd—the equivalent of two companies—occupying slots in the Plans and Operations shop, at the parachute rigging facility, in the motor pools, and elsewhere. Current army doctrine on the subject is that women can take jobs that do not imply direct combat, although they may have to fight if the local situation were to deteriorate. The women in the division are mostly airborne qualified, and do PT and the jumps with their units. Just the same, there is still some resentment about them. One officer remarked, "If

A C-130 delivers a Sheridan armored vehicle to the vicinity of notional combat. It is a very rapid way to deliver hardware, when you need it in a hurry.

we go to war, there go two companies before the first shot is fired, 220 people lost from combat." Others see it differently; they say that there are always people in the rear areas supporting the troops, and there is no reason to prevent women from participating there. There is also some resentment about the army's lower standards for women. The men who object to them say that in a combat situation there will be only one set of rules—those offered by the enemy—and people who can't perform effectively will endanger the mission of the unit. It is still a topic for argument,

66

but incidents over the years have converted some of the skeptics; several women have become the Honors Graduate of their Airborne Basic class. Others simply dig in and do their jobs in a professional manner.

Fire departments have three shifts, with one on and two off, and the 82nd does things in a similar way. One infantry brigade and one of its three battalions are always on call for immediate deployment, always at a high state of readiness for combat. The first airplane must be off the ground in less than eighteen hours from notification, a readiness that is tested frequently in emergency deployment readiness exercises, called "EDREs." These readiness exercises put the troops out the door and in the aircraft with weapons and ammunition and the full expectation that they are going someplace to fight. Usually, somebody tells them it is just another EDRE; sometimes, as on 25 October 1983, they go to war.

The bell that rings for this fire department is a complicated one. Only one person can make the call that sends these men to work, and that is the president of the United States in his role as commander in chief. It is always the president who takes responsibility for the commitment of armed men to the business of war. It is not a casual decision and he doesn't make it without a lot of help.

The president orders the secretary of defense to action, and the secretary and his minions begin to scurry. The consequence is a series of documents that order the division to action. The first is a warning order, which is used throughout the structure of the army to prepare organizations for possible action. In the case of the 82nd, this order would allow the staff to assemble plans, units, and equipment suited to the mission. Another consequence of this warning order is to isolate the selected units from the rest of the world.

Division staff have a vast library of scenarios and contingency plans to draw on during times of crisis. An assault on the Kremlin in January would require a different set of uniforms, equipment, maps, and the like than, say, a jump into downtown Havana in July. The planners are crucial people; they read newspapers with more thoroughness than you or I, because, from a planner's point of view, the crises on the front page represent the "help wanted" classifieds.

The orders from the president continue down through a chain of command from the secretary of defense; Joint Chiefs of Staff; commander of the 18th Airborne Corps, of which the 82nd is a part; to the commander of the division. Finally, a secret message form is received that reads: "THIS IS AN EXECUTE ORDER BY AUTHORITY AND DIRECTION OF THE SECRETARY OF DEFENSE." It describes the situation and refers to previous plans and options: COURSE OF ACTION: OPTION TWO IS APPROVED. 82ND AIRBORNE DIVISION CONDUCTS PARACHUTE ASSAULT 180210L OCT INTO SAN LORENZO; SECURES AIRHEAD AND FLIGHT LANDING STRIPS; RECEIVES FOLLOW ON AIRLAND; CONDUCTS MOVEMENT TO CONTACT TO THE EAST TO DESTROY ANTI SAN LORENZAN GUERRILLAS AND MACAPAN FORCES; CONDUCTS LINK UP WITH SAN LORENZAN FORCES AND CONDUCTS OPERATIONS TO RESTORE SOVEREIGNTY. MACAPAN GUERRILLA ACTIVITY VICINITY DROP ZONES.

This particular execute order is called "notional" and was used for a division-sized exercise;

67

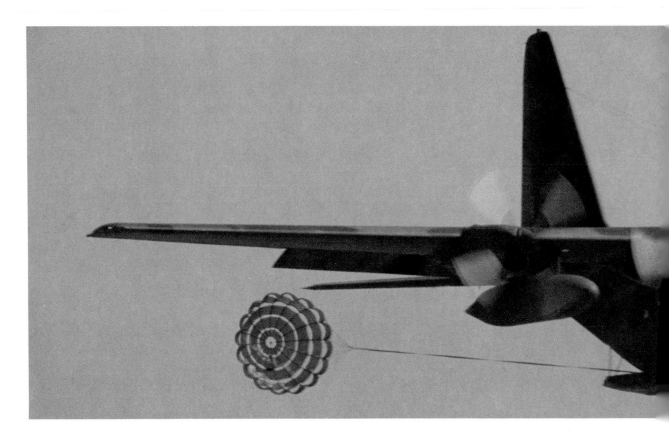

the contents for a real-world deployment would be quite similar but for a change in names.

Although the schedule is based on the concept of an N+18 hours wheels up on the first bird in the lead element, it can be done faster (thirteen hours for Grenada) or slower, extending to several days if appropriate. All the activities of each man are based on the ticking of the clock, and as time slips by, the units move toward their aircraft and their destiny.

Several hours after notification, the rigging of vehicles and heavy equipment for the lead element begin. The rigging facility is a large warehouse set up for just this purpose, and the riggers swarm over, under, and around the guns and trucks. A procession of vehicles await their turn and emerge in curious bondage, with shock-absorbing material, straps, and padding everywhere. You have to look twice to recognize the identity of the vehicle under all that stuff.

It is strictly a come-as-you-are affair. Since the nature of the mission can be almost anything from urban combat to antiguerrilla or antitank warfare, the kind of equipment needed can be exceedingly varied. During the deployment process, the commander will specify what everybody takes by

Drogue chute deployed, a C-130 descends to the airhead. Properly executed, the load exits about ten feet above the ground, and lands with a loud thud, but in one functional piece.

publishing a Minimum Mission Essential Equipment list (MMEE), which includes or omits items such as extra night-vision goggles, Dragon missiles, and radios. It is common, however, for subordinate commanders to plead for more of certain items they feel they can't live without. This extra equipment can come from storehouses or from units that aren't going on the mission. The pleading is discouraged, however, and if the division expects much follow on, they are not about to ransack one unit to build up another, or the donor could find itself without even MMEE.

As a fire department sends out only the appa-ratus and people suitable for each emergency, the 82nd deploys what it calls "force packages." Their deployment is based on a building-block concept, and four basic and different task organizations.

The first is the whole division, 15,000 para-troopers, configured in three infantry brigades, each brigade containing three infantry battalions. The battalions each contain five companies—four infantry and one anti-armor. Division artillery

(DIVARTY) goes with three battalions, one to support each infantry brigade. There is also an aviation brigade and several other battalions and smaller elements, including engineering, communications, and a company of military police, that are separate from the basic infantry brigades.

The second organization is a brigade task force. There are three infantry brigades in the division, so each one takes a turn as the on-call brigade. The on-call brigade becomes the Division Ready Brigade (DRB) One, and its 3,500 people are, as they say, good to go. Within the DRB 1 are three battalions, known as Division Ready Force 1, 2, and 3. In the event of an emergency, they deploy in order.

Within the brigade task force are three battalions, one of which is always designated as the first to go to war. That battalion, with its 1,000 or so paratroopers, becomes the Division Ready Force One (DRF 1) — the third task organization.

The result of this arrangement is that the division always has people on guard, ready to slide down the pole and go off to the fire. It also means that other people are able to train and do maintenance without having to worry about being called out in the middle of the night. They can still be called out, but it will be for a bigger fire and they will have a lot of company. When push really comes to shove, the whole division deploys by brigades, in sequence, from separate airfields.

These designations are important as foundations, but they're not entirely gospel and they're

A UH-60 Blackhawk performs delivery service for division artillery. The Blackhawk is a strong, fast, multi-purpose beast that has significantly improved the combat effectiveness of the army.

often tinkered with. For example, each of these basic building blocks can be packaged with or without a variety of additional resources, resulting in light, medium, and heavy designations for the DRB and the DRF.

As the Division Ready Brigade and Division Ready Force are assembled, they grow in complexity and in capability. Communications, weapons, artillery, engineers, counter battery radar, helicopters, antiair missiles, and armor can all be added as required. Individually, each of these elements is impressive; collectively, arrayed for battle, they are awesome. The commander has to decide what to take and what to leave, praying he makes the right choices from all the possible options and limitations that the real world imposes on armies and commanders. But that is what a commander is hired to do, and he better like the job or find another.

There is a great deal more to the business of deployment than bundling up all the people and their tools and tossing them into airplanes. Perhaps the most critical moments in any assault are the first ones, particularly for airborne. To be successful in combat requires the application of overwhelming force on an enemy before he applies overwhelming force on you. Airborne and air assault operations are vulnerable to many hazards, which begin before the jumpers land on the drop zone. Those initial minutes, as people and weapons and vehicles slam into the enemy's ground, must go well if the force is to prosper. And to go well on the drop zone, the contents of the aircraft must be loaded in a sequence that anticipates the needs of the battle.

The concept the 82nd uses is called "echelonment" — a system of organizing the units as they outload so they arrive in a manageable and tactical

Prestart checklist complete, the foundation of the Airborne, Lockheed's legendary C-130 Hercules meets the dawn, ready for another mission. This one will be to put jumpers into the air 1,250 feet above Fryar Drop Zone at Fort Benning.

The CH-47 Chinook began doing this kind of thing in 1964 as part of the experiment in airmobility and assault called the 11th Air Assault Division. The helicopter and the concept were both successful.

sequence. There are three components to this concept.

The first is the *assault echelon,* identified as ALPHA/BRAVO. These are the first elements to enter the objective area, and they include the combat and combat support elements, with perhaps the command posts for the brigade and division. They secure the drop zone and may move off to other objectives.

The second component, the *follow-on* (or CHARLIE) *echelon,* arrives as soon afterward as the USAF and the tactical situation will permit. The follow-on echelon supports the assault echelon. It also includes headquarters from the units.

The last element is the fabled *rear echelon,* who traditionally may never hear the sounds of guns. The army has a term for these clean, safe people who share the glory of the division without (the assault element thinks) sharing the risks. The word is REMF. The first two letters stand for "rear echelon" and the other two you'll have to make up because this is a family show. They are the DELTA echelon. Even with the 82nd, there are administrative and logistical jobs to be done, and somebody has to do them. In this kind of warfare, the rear may be very far away indeed.

All of these elements can be (and are) mixed and matched as situation or accident determines, and DELTA folks may find themselves floating through a hostile sky with the first stick of the first serial on the first DZ.

The division uses two ways of putting people on the ground, and often the commander will have a choice between the two. Jumping gets a lot of people on the ground in a hurry, but they tend to be spread around and mixed together. There are also long, anxious moments while the assault troops climb out of their harnesses, check for fractures or bullet wounds, and then try to find the assembly area. It takes a while, and it is a vulnerable while. Much effort is expended in preparing some of the artillery for immediate fire missions, from the drop zone itself, as a defense. Airland, on the other hand, puts a planeload of people out all together, complete and undamaged, with leaders and equipment intact, if a suitable spot is handy.

The decision is based on the kind of mission, the size of the objective, the situation of the bad guys, the availability of airports, the size of the force being delivered, whether or not a staging base will be used, and how many airframes there are to work with. The lead elements can expect to be rigged to jump, but the airplanes will be landed as soon as possible, delivering their contents out the back, which makes for a more efficient use of the aircraft.

All of these structures and scenarios exist because the airborne/air assault force still has an important place in the world of crisis management and conflict resolution. Compared to conventional forces, the airborne deploys almost instantly and doesn't need seaports, beaches, or airfields. That is the basic advantage of airborne ops.

The flip side traditionally has been logistics. It is easier to put an airborne force in the field than to keep it in the field. All of the army is talking these days about the "tooth-to-tail ratio," the comparison between the fighting part of a unit and the nonfighting, support part. Even the 82nd has a tail, and it can be a long one. Units in combat consume vast supplies of ammunition and MREs and all the other consumables required for a camping trip in the wilds. It has to come from somewhere, and that's the logistic side of the assault. When the air force delivers the troops, it turns around and goes back for the groceries and gasoline. As long as there are units in the field, there will be an organization attempting to get them their supplies. If that organization fails, the assault is doomed, despite the resolve of the ALPHA/BRAVO echelon. That is one disadvantage of airborne ops.

Another is that a lightweight infantry division, far away from its friends, is vulnerable to armor. Tanks today are remarkable beasts, with high-tech armor and weapons systems that are downright dangerous. Tanks are the favorite target of everybody on the battlefield and those above it, too. They can be defeated, but it isn't often easy or cheap, and the resources of the 82nd are not designed to go head to head with a lot of armor. But emergencies that call the division out of the firehouse are not tailor-made for the personal preferences of the firefighters. They may have to fight armor, and they may get chewed on in the process. Both logistics and armor threats are problems for the 82nd, and they have some solutions for both. One solution is a large supply of fire-breathing Dragons and TOW missiles, both

of which can kill armor on the battlefield. Another is a friendly relationship with the United States Air Force, particularly the men who drive the A-10 close air support aircraft that orbit the battlefield like large green vultures, hoping for something to pounce upon.

The relationship of the 82nd to the air force is a close and dependent one in transport, combat support, and logistics. The immense airplanes that deliver the troops to battle and go back and return with supplies make deliveries in spectacular ways. Three methods are used.

The first is a container system that can handle anything weighing up to 2,200 pounds that can be put on a pallet. These containers can drop supplies and equipment to within 225 meters of a designated spot. One C-141 can carry up to forty of these bundles and can cruise around the airhead dropping one or more on each pass over the DZ wherever they're needed.

Another delivery method is called Low Altitude Parachute Extraction (LAPES), which represents a dramatic technique for putting heavy, bulky equipment on the ground in a hurry. A C-130 makes a very low pass over any fairly flat and unobstructed terrain (a road, for example) that is at least 50 meters wide and 1,100 meters long. With the cargo doors open, a small drogue parachute appears and stabilizes; next a large drogue appears and deploys; then, out of the back appears a massive load, such as a Sheridan tank or a bulldozer or a lifetime supply of 105mm

howitzer ammunition, just five or ten feet above the ground. It hangs there for an instant before gravity does its job, and the load slams to the ground in a satisfying cloud of dust and noise. It is immediately attacked by a mob of troops who strip it of its bonds. In the case of a vehicle, the engine is started and it is off the DZ before the plane is out of sight. It's a wonderful system and almost always works; but the troops delight in stories of those rare and memorable moments when things don't go quite right, and a big expensive piece of technology makes a large hole in the dirt.

Another system that can also fail spectacularly (on rare occasions) is the Heavy Equipment Airdrop System. If you attach enough canopies to something you can probably drop it from an airplane and have it land intact, and that's the basic theory here. The riggers use 100-foot parachutes and deploy them with precision timing devices to dump equipment such as bulldozers and earth movers onto the DZ; when these systems fail, it can be quite entertaining. In fact they are pretty exciting to watch when they work properly, too, which is almost all the time, although it seems to take forever for the canopies to open, and the hardware is often about halfway to the ground before deployment is complete.

It helps to have blue skies for airborne operations, but of course, the weather isn't reliable. It used to be that pilots required a minimum of a 1,500-foot ceiling and three miles of visibility before they'd drop by to visit the airhead. That's pretty good weather for some likely travel destinations. Northern Europe gets about 2.3 days of sunshine a year, and you can bet it won't be the days you need them. Consequently, some of the air force C-130s have an Adverse Weather Aerial

Left: Most military parachutists are afraid of *not* being allowed to jump. This fashionably attired trooper is wearing about 110 pounds of assorted accessories, and the stuff gets heavier and more uncomfortable the longer you wear it. Let me at that door!

The OPFOR gets a dusty little strip for its tactical operations during Market Time, just like what it will probably get the next time the bullets fly.

Delivery System that permits navigation in "zero/zero" weather to a DZ and delivery of the goods under any conditions except high winds.

These new technical developments have changed tactical doctrine. An airhead used to be ten to twenty klicks across—six to twelve miles; it is now thirty to sixty kilometers. The old airhead was based on the notion that a fixed linear defense or perimeter was required for safety, and a ring that size was as big as a division could manage. The divisions had to protect their drop zones for resupply and for logistical bases from which to fight. The new system for delivering supplies frees up the division from its drop zones and allows it to spread out and antagonize the bad guys, getting ammunition and all the other supplies wherever and whenever required.

The other major disadvantage of air assault—the vulnerability to armor—is approached in several philosophical ways. The first is to acknowledge that it is a limitation. The division isn't set up to fight armor in a big way. It expects to be abrasive to armored or mechanized forces if it is on the kind of terrain that favors defense against tanks, but there are places where the division would do poorly against that kind of force. The logistic advantages provided by aerial resupply make it possible for airborne units to make it tough for armor to beat, but they all know life is short, and it can be shorter.

As the division says in its executive summary:

We do not intend to hold a fixed line, nor do we expect to eject the enemy force from the Main Battle Area. A fixed linear defense, built principally around machine guns and designed primarily to fight other infantry, fails to take advantage of what the Antitank Guided Missile can and cannot do; it also subjects our forces to massed conventional fires. Instead we intend to decimate a more mobile enemy who is forced to enter our defensive sector. To do this, we must deploy the Division on terrain or critical objectives that eliminate as many enemy options as possible, forcing him to fight on ground of our choice. Only by placing infantry with ATGMs in depth on armor restrictive terrain can we capitalize on the firepower available to us. With an antiarmor capability of 54 Sheridans, 162 ground TOW systems, 276 Dragon systems, 48 TOW Cobra helicopters, unlimited LAWs and antitank mines, plus air force, navy and marine fighter aircraft, we have a respectable ability to combat armor for a limited amount of time.

The division has two principal worries about all this: that it must be on ground that favors the way it fights armor, and that if it gets stuck in a big fight with other units alongside, the other units don't mess things up by going into a linear defense or an active defense, both of which would result in a goatscrew for the 82nd when those big clankers come over the ridge.

So, generally, the 82nd has a full set of virtues and vices as a military organization, as does every other. It moves to the battle quickly and is effective when it arrives. It is difficult to keep supplied and safe when armor is part of the picture. It has some other limitations, though; it needs more air support than a normal infantry division. It has no big guns of its own, although its parent, 18th Airborne Corps, does, which makes it harder to provide counterfire and suppress enemy air defense artillery. If corps guns show up on the airhead, this is no longer a problem. Then too, it is not the most mobile force in the world once it gets on the ground. Most of the maneuver battalions walk to work, and the helicopters available within the division can lift the assault elements of only two companies at a time. On top of that, it is at the mercy of the air force for delivery to battle and supply until things get quite conventional.

Jumpers load onto a C-130. First man in is last man out.

79

Fire and Maneuver

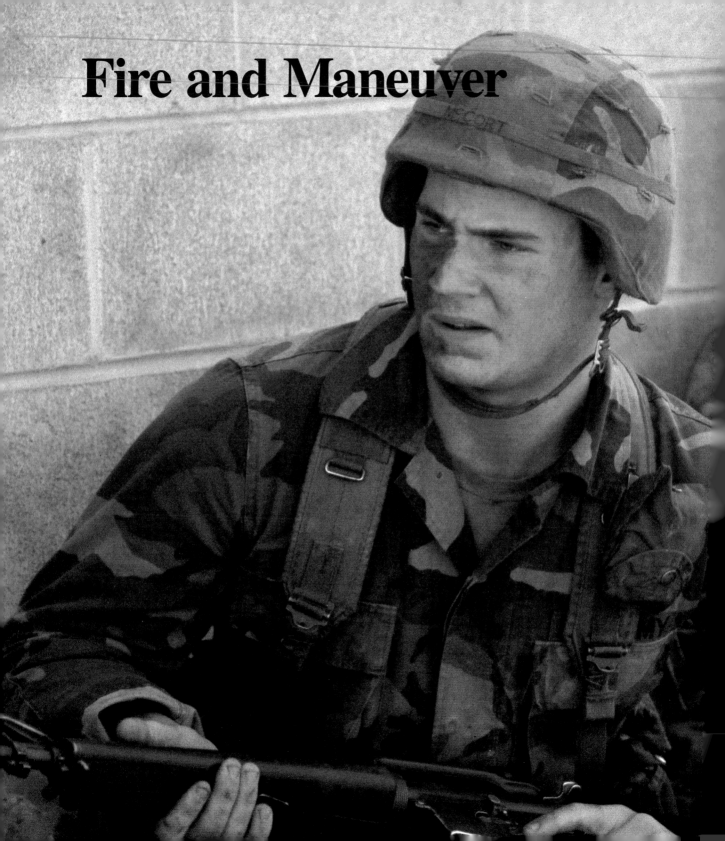

The 82nd Airborne Division is like a huge traveling circus, with many acts to rehearse and refine, each to be performed within the context of a larger show. It is also like improvisational theater, in that nobody ever knows exactly where, when, or what kind of audience will see the show, or how the various acts will need to interrelate while they perform their death-defying routines. So the only way for the performers to feel even a little confident is to rehearse, and rehearse, and rehearse.

In the middle of the night, in the middle of a holiday weekend, the whistle will blow and the units will start pulling in the troops. A soldier celebrating an anniversary with his wife will show up in formation with the rest, but he may be in his tuxedo while they are in jeans. Often, they are dismissed after the roll is called. Other times, it's into BDUs and LBE (load bearing equipment), draw your weapons from the arms room, and get down to Green Ramp.

Sometimes the whole division goes to the field with plenty of notice, off to explore the nether regions of Fort Bragg for a couple of weeks. These full-scale exercises are more challenging for the planning staff and commanders than for the troops. These big exercises mean huge mass tactical drops, with thousands of troops and all their gear dropping onto the drop zones out back. The coordination involves far more than the 82nd and includes navy, marines, and air force units. It is played from a scenario designed to simulate the real world as much as one of these exercises can. And, just like the real world, it begins with an execute order that orders the division to battle. Now the play begins. For this full-dress performance, the audience is primarily the division itself, along with its parent, 18th Airborne Corps.

This order represents official notification, and the time it is received becomes important in the sequence of events that follows. The division headquarters (in the personage of the Assistant Chief of Staff, G3) establishes the N hour and the clock begins to tick a countdown. The elements of the division have a series of activities that must be done on a schedule beginning with that official time. Personnel are recalled, formed up, accounted for; weapons are drawn, ammunition and MREs issued. While the troops and their company commanders are collecting their gear, the senior commanders and staff meet for a final and crucial meeting at headquarters. The meeting is held two hours after notification, in a large conference room called the N Plus Two room: this briefing coordinates all the decision makers for the final time before they, too, go off to draw weapons and ammunition.

The N Plus Two room can accommodate about a hundred people, and does for this conference. The leaders assemble and quietly conspire, waiting for the boss. The ones who will be going already have faces camouflaged and wear their LBE. For real-world missions, the atmosphere is as tense and tight as backstage on Broadway on opening night. A captain steps through the door, comes to attention, and says, "Gentlemen, the division commander." The room is totally silent for a moment as he enters. "Take your seats," he invites rather than commands. They sit. The briefing is extremely formal and goes in exact

---

Previous pages: Two troopers rehearse their roles in a little play called "Military Operations in Urban Terrain" at Fort Bragg's MOUT site.

sequence. Although a hundred people pack the room, it is silent except for the ritual of the brief and the occasional question or comment from the division commander or the airborne commander.

The briefers from the G2 Section (Plans and Operations) produce their maps and diagrams; one soldier uses a pointer to indicate the critical features while another recites the information.

This is the standard prologue to any scenario. It happens every time. What follows varies tremendously in detail from one scenario to the next. Some assumptions are made based on previous plans, on SOP, on all sorts of things. If you happen to be the division commander, you will hear something like this:

All the way, sir! I am Major Lossius from G3 Operations. On 5 January 1987 the pro-U.S. country of Buentipos severed diplomatic relations with Maltipos, a Marxist country governed by a military dictatorship. Political differences and recent cross border incursions have led to a buildup of Buentipan and Maltipan military forces along the border. Buentipos, invoking the mutual defense treaty of 1960, requested direct U.S. assistance should Maltipan forces invade. On Wednesday, 7 January, a cross border artillery fire exchange between Maltipan and Buentipan army units occurred.

Sir, at 0500 this morning a Maltipan cross border attack resulted in the National Command Authority directing the Joint Chiefs of Staff to involve U.S. military forces in support of Buentipos. The JCS Execute Order to C-in-C South was retransmitted by XVIII Airborne Corps to the 82nd Airborne Division at 0855 this morning. N hour for the division was established at 090900 ROMEO January 1987, with D day, P hour of 100500 ROMEO January '87 in the objective

area. The division will execute OPORD 6-87.

Although the names of the countries are "notional," the rest of the briefing sounds exactly like a real-world event; this is, after all, a rehearsal. Other briefers take the podium and add their particular bits of information.

One person is supposed to be on top of it all — the airborne commander. He has delegated many people within the division to work for him as his representatives; now, they put all the directives and policies and training to work.

There are four phases to an airborne operation:

- **Mounting,** which includes all the planning, assembling, and marshaling of people and weapons and airframes.
- **Air movement,** which begins with wheels up and ends when the last jumper exits the last aircraft over the drop zone.
- **Assault** phase, which begins with the first PLF on the DZ and ends when the initial airhead is consolidated.
- **Operations** phase, during which the force gets with the program and accomplishes its mission.

After notification the units go into isolation — nobody gets to call home to say they'll be late for dinner. You can tell things are happening at Bragg when everybody decides to go into their units at three in the morning. Then the place gets very quiet and nobody seems to be home. That's a good time to see what's cooking on the radio and television news.

A good person to watch during this period is a jumpmaster. The airborne commander appoints one for each aircraft; each is delegated command authority over all the jumpers aboard and each is responsible for the army equipment brought

82nd Airborne soldiers wait for the "cattle cars" that will take them to Green Ramp and a jump into a three-week field exercise.

along. As the commander's representative, the jumpmaster has considerable responsibility and the power to enforce it. it is up to these jump-masters to meet the eighteen-hour deadline for wheels up on the first bird. The jumpmaster is assisted in this formidable task by assistant jumpmasters, stick leaders, and "safeties," who take up some of the load of the process. The jumpmaster can delegate his authority but not his *responsibility;* if something goes wrong, it will be his fault.

His work begins in his unit area with a briefing from the Operations and Training officer (S3), from whom he is given the mission and the ground tactical plan, the air-movement plan, and infor-mation about the people who will assist him and when they can be briefed. He is told the time and place of the initial and final manifest calls and where and when prejump training can be done.

84

He is told when he'll be able to inspect the troops' uniforms and equipment and where and when parachutes will be issued. He'll be told about weather decision times, aircraft locations and tail numbers, and chalk numbers. He'll find out what the load time is, when the pilot/jumpmaster briefing will be, the station time, takeoff time, flight plan and drop time, and communications procedures on the DZ. All this in about ten minutes.

He then finds a quiet spot (if possible) to do a little paperwork: he organizes the people and equipment inside the plane into a collection called a "chalk." This ensures that when people and weapons land on the DZ they will be where they are supposed to be relative to the tactical plan. There are large, odd-shaped loads that some of the troops will drag out into the blast with them — Dragon missiles and CWIEs (container weapons and individual equipment) that must be cross-loaded — and the stick of jumpers has to be de-

Jumpmaster Personnel Inspection (JMPI) precedes every jump.

signed to accommodate the awkwardness of these loads.

Then, he holds a roll call to make sure he knows who's going on the mission. Those with the lumpy gear are told where they fit into the stick; then their equipment is inspected. This equipment and the containers are normally prepared for deployment at all times, so there should not be any frantic scurrying around now; but there probably will be some, anyway.

The jumpmaster briefs the troops on the details of the operation: the DZ, aircraft information, times, and all the rest. He passes on what he's heard from S3. The tactical side of the briefing comes from the platoon leaders and company commander.

The jumpmaster runs everybody through a little refresher training, which can include a few PLFs for everybody, off a platform or a picnic table. At minimum it reviews the Five Points of Performance that were hammered into every skull back at the Basic Airborne Course, a discussion of chute malfunctions and the proper use of the reserve, and what to do if you should become a towed jumper.

On that note, the jumpmaster dashes off to the departure airfield, leaving the rest of the troops to get together their kits. At the field he searches for and finds another one of the airborne commander's closest personal friends, the departure area control officer. The DACO is the man with the upset tummy. He has the job of setting up the foundation for the operation, making sure that all planes are present and accounted for, ready for loading. He provides the jumpmaster with an update briefing and any changes in the times, operational plan, weather, winds, or aircraft parking. The jumpmaster gives the DACO a copy of the jump manifest, with a copy for the aircraft commander. Then he sends one of the safeties off to inspect the aircraft that will carry him and his charges off to battle.

With the air force loadmaster, the safety inspects the aircraft around the doors from which the jumps will be made, checking for air deflectors and jump platforms, a secure anchor line, and a clean floor. Does the static line retriever system work? Seats okay? Caution lights work? Comfort pallets installed? Toilet paper in the latrine? Barf bags available? Nothing related to the efficient execution of the mission escapes him.

While the safety is busy with these chores, his jumpmaster leads the chalk off to get their parachutes and required air items. About an hour before station time the troops pair off into "buddy" teams and start chuting up. If the flight will be a long one, the chutes will be on the airplane and rigging and inspection will be done in flight. The gear is tolerable for a while, but nobody enjoys that kind of constraint for more than a couple of hours.

Once people are rigged, the inspection process begins. Four stations are usually used, with the jumpmaster at one, the assistant at another, and the safeties each manning one. A fifth station takes care of major deficiencies that will take more than a minute to fix. If the airframe happens to be a C-141, the chalk can be an entire company, 122 jumpers, each of whom must be checked for nineteen major areas of equipment. They start at the helmet and finish in proper sequence with the lowering line that is attached to the jumper's ruck and weapon container. This is usually done away from the aircraft, near the parachute issue point, preferably where there is good light and a place for the troops to wait in relative comfort. Then, when everybody has been inspected, the jumpmaster leads the group off to the aircraft, to arrive at the scheduled load time and with the scheduled station time (everybody aboard and ready for takeoff) clearly in mind. The parachute issue point and the aircraft may be separated by several hundred yards, and it can be rather unpleasant to waddle along in a lot of gear, but that is the way it is done, and in a closed formation, column of twos, when necessary.

Jumpmasters and their associates are under tremendous pressure at times like this, and the stresses of preparing for a jump can encourage people to cut corners and "drive on." To counter such pressures, there are a set of cardinal rules that are always supposed to be in the conscious mind of each jumpmaster, assistant, and safety. The first of these rules is: *never sacrifice safety for speed*. It is a noble rule, but jumpmasters will tell you that you had better be *both* safe and fast or the

Jumpers exit from 1,250 feet in a mass tactical drop.

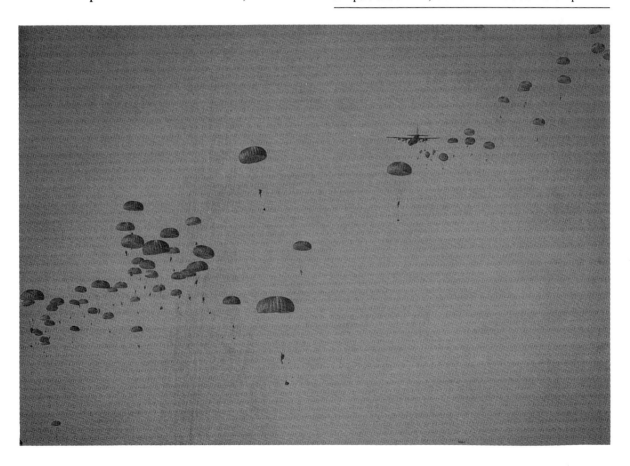

airborne commander will be looking for a new jumpmaster.

The jumpers load in reverse order—first in, last out—with the jumpmaster checking to ensure the sticks stay in proper sequence. Then the pilot and the jumpmaster huddle for a preflight briefing about revised takeoff time, drop time, and when the jumpmaster can expect a call from the air force combat control team or DZ safety officer for an update on conditions on the ground. They go over the SOP on in-flight procedures for the troops, the approach to the DZ, and what to do in emergencies. The clock continues to tick toward the eighteen-hour mark, and at the appointed instant the ground crew fires up their APU (auxiliary power unit); power flows to the bird. A crewman is positioned off the nose of the aircraft, waiting for the signal that the time has come. The aircraft commander nods. The crewman points to the Number One engine and signifies all clear and safe to start; in the cockpit the Number One engine start switch is depressed and the whine of the hydraulic system fills the whole aircraft as the compressor turbine starts its spin. At about 2,000

revolutions per minute the engine control opens a valve and a metered amount of JP5 is sprayed into the now-pressurized combustion chamber, where it encounters the white-hot tip of a glow plug; it lights with a soft flash and the engine begins to come to life, singing the lovely song of a big turboprop warming up. The sound and smell of the engines fill the cabin, vibrate into the seat frames, into the consciousness of every man aboard but particularly those who will not land with it. It is station time and time to go. It is N Plus Eighteen.

Meanwhile, in a notional country somewhere, far away . . .

It is a lovely evening, with a half moon and warm breezes coming in from the sea to cool a tropical landscape. The scene would seem peaceful, but there is tension in the air. Rumors, reports, orders, activity. The NCOs look preoc-

An infantry squad emerges from a smoke screen to assault the bleachers at a CAPEX (capabilities exercise), a demonstration for friends and families held annually at Bragg.

A TOW missile crew looks for targets. The missile is a wire-guided device that is steered by the gunner for a mile or so until it makes a hole in somebody else's armor-plated plans for the future.

cupied and intense; only the sentries walk their posts with their usual boredom. Nothing is so calculated to produce brain death as a guard mount almost anywhere on earth. There have been alerts and stand downs. Ammunition has been issued, then retrieved, then issued again. The rumors of invasion have been heard so often that they are now almost discounted, but not quite. The air defense battery on the hill is manned, but the soldiers are sprawled around the mount, talking casually among themselves. It is another night, another alert. The papers have been full of the usual government warnings about the possibility of an invasion by the United States, but then they always are. It is too nice a night to worry about it.

Far off in the distance, lightning flashes and the sound of tropical thunder filters across the miles. Gradually, softly, odd sounds grow in volume; at first, few hear them. Then, growing, they are heard but not identified. Then, they are heard and identified as the sound of jet engines growing in pitch and power in a way this ground has never heard. Then, all hell breaks loose.

Gun emplacements are enveloped in white fire and dust as the long, ripping bursts of 20mm high explosive incendiary rounds rain down from the sky. Even in the darkness, positions are struck by unseen but clearly heard aircraft. The noises grow in volume, variety, and intensity as rockets, bombs, bullets, and cannon fire sizzle into the fortifications and the vehicles at the edge of the airfield. The sounds echo and mix with each other. They are joined by new sounds from the ground—light, medium, and heavy automatic weapons pumping their bullets skyward. Tracers light the night with red and green lines of fire, green going up, red coming down. The big AAA battery with its radar fire-control van explodes; bits and pieces of the complex and carefully maintained Soviet technology now rain from the sky, just so much trash.

The barrage continues for what feels like an eternity for those who survive. The sky begins to lighten and the sounds change again as the procession of fighters withdraws; then a new sound—jet engines once again. A parade of airplanes approaches in trail formation. While the defenders stare in amazement at the stately procession, they see a new set of fighters appear just above the deck, squirming and swooping as they patrol the area below the huge cargo planes. Rolling inverted, arcing like playful porpoises, the fighters escort the defenseless transports. Bright flares shoot at intervals from the jets—decoys for any heat-seeking missiles that might be sent aloft.

Looking vertically, a surviving defender (and there are many) may observe the first C-130. From both doors, small objects fall away at one-second intervals, drop momentarily, then pause beneath olive nylon canopies that lower their riders to the airfield. The small objects are the most dangerous weapons on the battlefield; they are men. There are hundreds of them, then thousands, arriving in a relentless, methodical sequence. The first ones are taken under fire by the defenders, who recover sufficiently to remember what they are supposed to be doing, and with the courage to stay and do it. But they don't last long.

That, with variations, is the script for any conventional airborne assault. The 82nd adds to this script a drop of heavy equipment, which the Rangers dispense with. There was no heavy drop on Grenada.

The airborne part of the operation merely gets the people and their tools to the job site. Then they begin work, pretty much like any other American infantry division. With any luck, they are blessed by the element of surprise; but regardless, they now proceed to find, fix, and destroy the enemy. These scenarios combine all the nasty things that the real world holds in store for the division, in Europe or Central America or the Middle East. There are armor, guerrillas, conventional forces, air assets, and sometimes gas, all used by the bad guys, all needing an effective defense. An aggressor force is pitted against a friendly force, using a scenario designed to wring as much out of people as can be done without killing a lot of them. In one recent exercise, the division opposed an armored force that also had infantry, helicopters, and guerrillas.

For this exercise, the curtain rises on the drop

A mixed bag of things that go bump in the night, and in the day, too. TNT, dynamite, blasting caps, det cord are all used by the engineers to build and take apart things.

zone with the arrival of the marines, who've been invited to the party with their Spectre AC-130 gunship. From 5,000 feet in the middle of the night, they arrive to prep the DZ with 20mm high explosive and white phosphorous. The sound from the guns arrives after the targets are engulfed in fire, and instead of bang-bang-bang, you hear ZZZIIIIPPPPP!!!!!!! as the multibarreled weapon hoses the old APC and tank hulks representing enemy armor that it acquires in its nightsight. Shortly thereafter, the first C-141 in a parade of aircraft arrives; the heavy drop begins, followed by the mass tactical drop. The large movers and shakers thump to the dirt just minutes before the troops.

When the 82nd jumps, it normally begins at night and the heavy equipment goes first. Along

with the artillery drop the huge earth-moving graders—18,000-pound monsters that look like they wouldn't even fit in an airplane—along with dump trucks and skip loaders. They float down under a cluster of huge, 100-foot-diameter canopies, then meet the ground with a tremendous thud. When the drops are made during daylight, the sight of these massive loads being extracted from the low-flying C-141s diving for the ground as the canopies inflate with a roar is enough to inspire awe. If the riggers have done their job, the chute disengages from the load and drifts to the ground. Frequently, though, the canopy stays attached and a breeze can pull the load over on its side.

On top of each piece of gear is a small light to warn the troopers (who will follow onto the drop zone), so they won't land on the equipment. When the personnel land on the drop zone, they quickly gather at their assembly points, marked by lights of various kinds and combinations. Soon, strobes, chemlights, and flashlights all wave and blink from the assembly points on the drop zone, and the units assemble and move out. Within a few minutes, 105mm howitzers are booming away from the middle of the DZ, firing at targets miles away.

When the 82nd or the Rangers make a mass tactical jump into a hot DZ, they prefer to do it low, at about 500 feet. On the ground, each soldier's first mission is to secure the airhead and suppress any opposition. Suppress opposition

Fire from a Marine Spectre gunship rains down on targets during a division exercise. This kind of fire support is essential for securing airheads; it worked well in Grenada, taking out all sorts of targets in support of the Rangers and others on the ground.

means to try to locate where the shots are coming from and then to kill or capture or rout the people doing the shooting. In ones, twos, and threes, all the jumpers assault the defenders as soon as they get out of their harnesses. The secured area becomes the airhead, which at first is only a few hundred meters across. The airhead is the foundation of the assault, providing resupply and reinforcement as well as a place to depart from when the time comes. For some missions, such as a rescue scenario, the airhead might not be developed much at all.

Once the bad guys split (one way or another), people go about the business of assembling in their proper units, or "establishing unit integrity." Then they go off on their assigned missions. A defensive perimeter is established while teams leave to capture ground or facilities. When the initial rush of adrenaline is used up, an interesting phenomenon occurs: men start falling asleep! In Normandy, about this time in the assault, soldiers started collapsing as if they had been shot. They'd be standing there, then wham, out on the ground. It was a situation for which no one was prepared, and it was serious. In Grenada as well, NCOs had

A soldier waits for his unit to move. He's carrying an empty LAW launcher; the LAW is used for busting bunkers and light armor—and heavy armor when you're lucky.

a difficult time keeping their troops awake at times, as the hours of sleeplessness, excitement, fatigue, and then comparative safety took their toll.

Depending on the situation, all sorts of things start happening. If an armored force of any consequence is likely to show up, the engineers use their heavy equipment to build bunkers and anti-tank defenses. They don't expect to stop an assault cold with one easy shot but to channel the tanks and vehicles into kill zones where they can be hurt badly by artillery and antitank missiles. When the survivors get too close, the defenders pull back to a second prepared set of positions, where they are engaged in new and overlapping kill zones. The troops occupying these positions carry a lot of anti-armor weapons: there are LAWs for close-in defense, and almost everybody seems to have one. There are TOW missiles for killing at a distance; there are Dragons for the middle ground; and helicopters, A-10s, F-14s, and F-16s overhead, looking for trouble. None of these resources is likely to beat a Pro Bowl team all by itself, but together they can create a lot of heartburn.

While the infantry rush off to secure the air-head and others depart on the mission of the moment, the engineers begin extracting their hardware from its bonds. Straps are released, ties cut away, engines started. A grader that was pulled over on its side by a canopy that failed to release looks like a total loss. But it is pulled

upright, oil is replaced in the engine, and it is fired up and good to go only two hours after the drop.

The infantry company is the foundation of the division and the army; it includes about 125 men in four platoons, each with four squads. They function as teams within teams, each with identities, loyalties, vices, and virtues. The basic infantry squad, army wide, has a leader and two fire teams. Seven of the men carry M-16s while four have M-203s (a combination of an M-16 and a grenade launcher); one man gets to hump the Dragon missile, which weighs thirty-five pounds. The platoon headquarters group adds to the team two machine guns, an artillery forward observer, and a radio operator. The 82nd's squad is smaller, at nine men. Two carry squad automatic weapons (SAWs) instead of M-16s.

Exercises are interesting in the way that orchestra or professional football rehearsals are interesting. You can see people practicing the moves, concentrating on the components of the score a little at a time. There is something synthetic about it, though, something not quite right. With an orchestra or a football team or a military unit, what happens in practice doesn't count in the real world. The real world has an audience; in the world of warfare, the audience is the other side — an enemy who is trying to kill you. In real combat, there are many factors that influence the outcome; fear of death and injury is one of the biggest. That fear is lacking in exercises. It is an important omission, but until we're willing to let the guys "live fire" at each other, that's the way it's going to be. There are systems that simulate live fire to a degree, using laser transmitters and receivers attached to weapons and to the players, but it isn't quite as dramatic when an electronic device says you've been hit as when someone near

---

Spotter of a sniper team in his "ghillie" suit. Made with strips of dyed burlap, it provides extremely effective camouflage.

and dear to you starts leaking his juices into the dirt.

But military units practice just the same, because that's the only option they've got. It is a learning time for the privates and the generals. The lessons of exercises for the commanders are subtle improvements in the ways they deal with the situations and encounters they'll see in real war. For the troops, it is a chance to encounter some of the stresses of real combat.

The units set up shop during exercises the same way they intend to in war, and they move around

Above: A Sheridan light armored vehicle. Not technically a tank, it serves many of the same functions, but can still be delivered by a C-130. *Right:* A sniper team in ghillie suits. Snipers use a target rifle to make one-shot kills a thousand meters from their carefully camouflaged position.

in an intense and competitive way. Part of the division plays the role of the OPFOR — the opposition forces; the rest are the good guys. It is a useful rehearsal for actual encounters for both sides. The OPFOR can feel the tactics and doctrine of the people they expect to fight; the friendlies can try out the skills that are supposed to work

against Warsaw Pact philosophies. The aggressors actually become aggressive, using Soviet tactics and doctrine as much as possible. Uniforms are adapted to look like those of the Warsaw Pact countries. The armor moves forward as opposition armor might, supported by opposition scout helicopters and gunships.

On the third or fourth day of the exercise, the curtain rises for the second act, the armor assault. The attack has begun. In the distance, tanks and APC are on the move, exploring the terrain, inflicting and taking hits, firing and maneuvering. Large units move against each other in the dark and smoke. Fatigue takes its toll. Tactics that worked well in smaller rehearsals disintegrate here.

The assault is moving toward our positions. The radio is alive with traffic and tension; you can hear the voices of the enemy on the battalion TOC radios:

GOLF SEVEN TWO, INDIA EIGHT TWO, I WAS REPORTING THE OBSTACLES BEING BREACHED, PROCEEDING ON TO "DART." I'VE GOT THE INFANTRY IN FRONT OF ME, THEY'RE LEADING MY TANKS, BREAK. I NEED ONE ENGINEER DUMP TRUCK OR ONE SQUAD OF ENGINEERS.

Their armor is moving forward, phase line to phase line, taking and inflicting casualties, buying ground with time and notional blood and destruction. We can hear them and they can hear us; there is jamming and counterjamming. They get past the obstacles, although the barriers slow them down, and are being channeled into the kill zones. You can hear them over the radio. Even though it is a rehearsal, it is a full-dress one. The voices of an enemy battalion commander and one of his company commanders are full of tension

and frustration as the assault runs into the wall the defenders have designed to contain them:

. . .ROGER EIGHT TWO, WE'RE GONNA TRY TO GET UP AND TAKE THAT HIGH GROUND, OVER.

WE HAVE BEEN IN HEAVY CONTACT, THEY'VE REPORTED NUMEROUS HEAVY CASUALTIES, OVER.

WHAT *KIND* OF CASUALTIES, OVER?

PEOPLE CASUALTIES, THEY'RE JUST BEING OUTNUMBERED, OVER.

YOU GONNA HAVE TO WITHDRAW, OVER?

AFFIRMATIVE, OVER.

The commander's voice becomes even more strained:

VICTOR EIGHT TWO, THIS IS GOLF EIGHT TWO, OVER.

The contemporary battlefield (at least the American version) requires good communications between the commander and the commanded, so one of the weapons is electronic. Jamming systems seek out and overpower the enemy's frequencies; these jamming systems and strategies don't kill anyone directly, but the confusion they produce helps break down the coordination and cohesion of the opposition force. Jamming is blocking the enemy commander from hearing the response, and he's getting testy.

VICTOR EIGHT TWO, THIS IS GOLF EIGHT TWO, OVER! PUSH YOUR TALK BUTTON AND TALK TO ME!

They have a variety of methods for evading the jamming, some of which work—sometimes. But on a battlefield that depends on clear secure comms, jamming is a significant hazard.

JULIET EIGHT TWO, GOLF EIGHT TWO, COME ON UP HERE ASAP, WHERE THE

"Are you *sure* that's where we're supposed to go?" A platoon leader ponders his options while waiting the next move.

Sergeant Meikle (Airborne, Ranger), veteran of the parachute assault on Point Salines, rehearses during more peaceful times at Fort Bragg.

SMOKE IS, COME TO THE SMOKE!! THEY GOT A WHOLE INFANTRY COMPANY DUG IN UP HERE!! THEY'RE MOVIN' TOWARD THOSE TANKS UP HERE!

He is nearly screaming now: WE NEED PROTECTION!!

The commander has taken all the casualties he can stand, and after a futile few minutes attempting to rally his remaining forces he tries to break contact.

The infantry is a tremendously flexible, powerful, and capable organization, in both offense and defense, but it isn't invulnerable. The way the airborne works leaves the infantry units somewhat vulnerable to a serious reaction from a capable adversary. Armor is traditionally the source of most heartburn for the ground pounder, and it takes only a few of the noisy critters to ruin your whole day.

The combat engineers of the 82nd have a lot to do: they construct fortifications, bridges, obsta-cles. To do their work they use a wide variety of explosives, heavy equipment, hand tools, their bare hands, and a lot of ingenuity.

As infantry divisions go, the 82nd isn't supplied with as much hardware and people as a conventional division, but it does get some important extra assets. It's supposed to be a high speed/low drag organization that moves into position fast and makes it possible for the rest of the team to catch up. It has a heavy supply of squad automatic weapons and M-203s; it alone uses the little Sheridan, which looks like a tank but is really an armored and tracked vehicle. It's lightweight, which makes it possible to eject from an airplane; but it's hardly a match, nose to nose, with a main battle tank. That's supposed to be all right though, because the Sheridan isn't supposed to be banging heads with big-time armor.

The division has fewer people, fewer vehicles, and fewer logistics resources than other conventional ground infantry divisions. So you could say, on paper and statistically, that the division is weaker. You could say that, but you shouldn't. The division has a mixture of resources that collectively make it one of the most potent meat grinders operated by any government anywhere. Some of its effectiveness is based on the way the physical and organizational resources are mixed, but the most important element is the character of the people. As one first sergeant says:

The average paratrooper is quite a bit different from guys in other units, like night and day. Not just what they knew and how they trained, but their attitude. They're a different type of individual, they really are. A whole different attitude than you have in other units: they're tough, they're good to their buddies, they're loyal. It is particularly apparent when you go away, you can pick the airborne guys out of a crowd. They are a cut above; they expect *to be a cut above!*

The strength of the division goes back to jump

A rifleman emerges from the fog of notional war at a CAPEX. The Dragon launcher he's carrying is *much* lighter when it is empty, as it is here. Less effective, too, but it looks good.

school and the attitude of self confidence and resourcefulness that every airborne soldier develops there. Airborne troops don't expect gentle treatment, so they plan for difficult times. They have learned to be adaptable, with their equipment, tactics, and expectations. It is just as well, for combat requires it.

The engineers have a whole collection of techniques for assisting the infantry to defeat an armored assault. There is no way for engineers to stop a serious large-scale assault, but there is a lot they can do as part of the team to make the advance too expensive to sustain.

Most battlefields have natural features that restrict movement of troops and vehicles. Roads and open terrain favor advancing elements, while hills and water can slow them. By constructing obstacles in the right places, a defender can force an attacker to enter a killing ground where defensive firepower has been focused. This is no news to the attacker, who has read the book himself, and the encounter will be like any competition where one set of strengths and weaknesses opposes another set with virtues and vices of its own.

Despite the way Rambo goes about it in the movies, you don't just grab an M-60 and win the war by charging up the hill. There are times when that is called for, and those guys are heros for sure. Their widows meet the president and he gives them the Medal of Honor. Human wave attacks are a technique for reducing your force in very short order, and it is not popular with the 82nd.

The army has philosophies about how to do business in the most efficient and economical way it can; the idea (as George Patton remarked) is not to give your life for your country but to make sure the other guy donates *his life* for the enemy country. To be effective and economical requires planning, coordination, and teamwork. In large-scale, conventional action, what you end up with is a 15,000-man football team that throws real "bombs." That team is built from many smaller teams that understand their role in the grand scheme. As the team goes to work, there are huddles at many levels, with the plays being carried down to the players. Everybody knows what the basic routines are; they practice them all the time. The playbooks are called *FM7-8* (*Infantry Platoon and Squad*) and *FC7-22* (*Infantry Squad and Platoon Drills*). The leaders receive their missions, then gather their troops and issue what is called a warning order:

Waiting to move. A SAW gunner in the field. The ammunition is in a plastic "assault pack" which may be thrown away in combat, but at Bragg you have to clean up after yourself.

When you've been going full tilt for two or three days without sleep, any momentary halt is a chance for rest, any pillow will do.

Our mission is to attack the town of Burg at 1430. The enemy has some good positions in the buildings. There may also be enemy tanks in the town. Draw six grenades for each man, and one LAW for each man. Each squad will carry ten blocks of C4, ten non-electric blasting caps, ten fuse lighters, a hundred feet of "det" cord, and ten feet of fuse. The platoon sergeant will tell you where and when you can pick it up. Let me know by 1145 if you have any problems with radios or weapons. Meet me back here at 1105. At that time, we will move to the ridge overlooking the town, where I will give the complete order.

The troops are briefed by their squad leaders, and then they all scurry about, getting their individual acts together. At the appointed hour, the leaders go off and conspire, preferably while looking at the terrain they will attack. The platoon leader describes the plan, called the complete order. He describes the situation of friendly and enemy forces, the mission to be accomplished, and how it is to be done. If they can, the troops rehearse fire and maneuver; immediate action drills; actions at the assault position; breaching mine fields; and clearing trenches, bunkers, and buildings.

Even the movement to contact with the enemy is done in a formalized way, depending on the kind of contact expected. When there is a good chance of banging into the enemy while moving, a technique called "bounding overwatch" is used to provide protection. One of the platoon's squads moves forward (up to 200 meters, the effective range of the M-16), while the others guard it from concealed positions. That squad then overwatches as the others bound forward using cover and concealment. This kind of movement is slow, but it makes for fewer casualties.

The 82nd constantly rehearses the skills needed for coping with ambushes, clearing fortified or urban areas, dealing with tanks, and defending positions. One of the techniques that Grenada encouraged was the use of "live fire" exercises, where units move and shoot with artillery rounds exploding nearby and with the blanks in their magazines replaced with ball ammunition. The 82nd has always used live fire exercises, but now they use them a great deal more. They assault positions and shoot as they are supposed to, with bullets and shrapnel in the air. Despite careful safety precautions, a live fire is potentially dangerous if people fail to fire and move as they have been trained. There are many people assaulting a position in squad, platoon, or company strength. There are a lot of bullets in the air. On rare occasions people are shot by accident and sometimes are killed, but the job they're practicing was never supposed to be completely safe. The idea behind the live fires is to develop moves that are dangerous to the bad guys while being safe to your own team.

AVIATION

There is a lot more to the 82nd than the infantry companies, although they are its foundation. There is a separate Air Cav regiment that provides a lot of services for the troops. They use four types of helicopters—the Chinook and the Blackhawk for hauling around people and equipment, the Cobra for attacking, and the OH-58 for scouting.

The Cobra/scout team is fascinating in action. Both fly in the treetops, zipping around in front of the troops. The Cobra is there to protect the scout, nothing else, during these recons. The scout uses terrain to hide, and sneaks as close as possible to the bad guys without getting hosed. When the enemy's strength and location are discovered, the details are sent back to the folks who need to know; then the information can be used to attack or defend against the opposition. If an enemy helicopter comes after the observer, the Cobra is there to wax his tail with guns or rockets. The Cobra has a crew of two—one to drive, the other to shoot. The gunsight is a lot more expensive than the ones on the M-16s; it's a stabilized and magnified scope that looks as though it belongs in an F-14. The gunner also has another aiming device—a sensor system that is connected to his helmet and points the guns where he's looking. The racks of TOW missiles on either side of the

A snake in the grass. A Cobra gunship hovers below the treeline for a few minutes. The Cobras support the OH-58 scout helicopters, protecting them from the forces of evil.

cockpit are useful when you want to stop someone who's riding around in a steel foxhole several thousand yards away.

The Blackhawks are becoming the workhorses of the division's air assets. They shuffle around 105mm howitzers, bring in hot chow, carry out the ARPs on their adventures behind enemy lines, and generally do the numerous things the old Huey used to do, only about three times better. The Blackhawk is fast, carries a lot of troops, has power up the kazoo, and is reliable.

The Chinook is an old warhorse, having hauled around guns, vehicles, and a lot of other things for the army for more than twenty years. It can take aboard part of a scout platoon, hook up to a 105mm howitzer and its ammo, and fly off into the sunset with the greatest of—well, that *is* actually stretching things a bit—but it can do it.

103

FIRE! A 155mm crew "pulls the tail" on their gun. They are from 18th Airborne Corps, rather than DIVARTY, but they play from the same sheet of music.

DIVARTY

Another one of the very best friends of the infantry is the artillery. Airborne operations impose limitations on what is and isn't suitable for use. Normal infantry gets lots of support from big guns that can create many problems for bad guys even when they are far away. The 82nd's artillery has fifty-four 105mm howitzers for what it calls "close-in" direct support. These guns will fire out to 11,500 meters—about six miles—at the rate of three rounds a minute.

The battery commander says: *The primary mission of the field artillery is to support the maneuver arm. In other words, I am a slave to an infantry battalion commander. I am his long arm of combat power. I shoot and kill the enemy at great ranges. In order to accomplish that mission, I have three primary units with my battery. The first is the Forward Observer, whose job it is to go out with the infantry, who can call back to me to tell me where to fire my bullets, and to tell me where the infantry is. They are the eyes of the field artillery.*

The second element is my Fire Direction Center, which is the "brains" of the field artillery. Their primary mission is to process all data coming in from whatever source, in order that we might effectively engage the enemy.

On the last day of a field period, the units start the road march back home. For some the trek begins at three in the morning because it's over twenty miles back.

The third element is the "brawn" of the field artillery, the muscle! The guns!

A field artillery battery is comprised of eighty men, and the fifth platoon, that supports the men, is comprised of thirty men, so there are a hundred and ten men in a field artillery firing battery. There are six M-102 105mm howitzers in each battery. They can launch a thirty-five pound projectile out to approximately 11,500 meters. The guns receive their data from the Fire Direction Center, which tells them what direction to point, how high to elevate their tubes, and what "charge" to fire to impact on the enemy. That's how the battery is organized.

The thing peculiar about the 82nd Airborne artillery is that it goes into the objective area at the same time the infantryman does. The division drops its howitzers out of airplanes into the same LZ where the troops land. There is a supply of ammunition with each gun, and within a short time—fifteen minutes in daylight, twenty minutes at night—the guns fire from the DZ.

"It really pumps the infantry up to land there on the drop zone," says the battery commander, " and just twenty minutes after the drop to hear BOOM! BOOM! BOOM! on the drop zone! That's big bucks for us as far as public affairs is concerned."

The battery is not stuck where it drops, but is almost as mobile as the troops. The vehicles that move the battery are dropped with the guns, and they can move around on roads or cross country. And, when a movement needs to be done in a hurry, the whole battery can be lifted by helicopters to a new firing position.

The battery commander is quietly confident about his unit: *This is* absolutely, without a doubt, the finest artillery firing battery in the world! *There are only nine American airborne artillery firing batteries in the world, nine here at Fort Bragg, and one in Vicenza, Italy, and without a doubt, Alpha Battery, First of the 319th Field Artillery, is NUMBER ONE! We work hard, we go to the field, we train hard; we all* want *to be here! We volunteered to jump out of airplanes, and it takes a special kind of guy to do that. We volunteered to be field artillerymen, something that nobody forced upon us, that we asked to do! There's a lot of pride and esprit in everything we do. We like to do well, and we do, in everything from sports to firing competitions! We take everything seriously, we're always competitive. You won't find another battery anywhere that can compare to Alpha battery!"*

And you can bet every other battery commander thinks the same thing about *his* battery!

Mortar crew reboards a helicopter after a fire mission. The men and all their equipment will be back in the air before the rounds they have just fired hit the target.

Urgent Fury

It wasn't black, and it wasn't white, but somewhere in that gray area we call "the real world." Like most of the problems that confront the people who govern, the way things were evolving was frustrating as hell. The questions were painfully obvious, like the essay problems in some fiendish graduate college course in international relations, but this was grad school of a different kind. This was the real world. Here's the story:

There is a little island in the Caribbean called Grenada. It's a scenic place, settled longer than the United States, discovered by Columbus in 1498. The population is black, the descendants of the slaves who once worked the nutmeg, sugar, and banana plantations. It is one of those many former British colonies that are now free, independent, and impoverished, a sovereign nation since 1974. It has a 50 percent unemployment rate and a sixty-five-man army. Like many other such islands, its politics are rather goofy, with a mixture of left wing themes and variations. But so what? It's none of our business, is it? There is a medical school on the island, with about a thousand American students attending three campuses. There are also a whole lot of Cuban military folk, Soviets, and a mixed bag of Eastern Europeans camped on Grenada; some of them are building a long runway for the new local airport, for tourist airplanes to come and visit, so they say. If it were as simple as that, or if it had simply stayed like that, there would never have been a problem. However . . .

On 13 October, the prime minister of the little nation is deposed and arrested by the Central Committee as part of a power struggle. He and several followers are placed under guard and house arrest in Saint George's, the capital.

On 17 October, the United States Defense and State departments consider ways to extract the 1,000 American students from the island through diplomatic means, and don't come up with any obvious solutions.

On 19 October, a crowd of between 10,000 and 15,000 supporters gather before the former prime minister's house, overwhelm the guards, and release the prime minister. He is transported to army headquarters at Fort Rupert, where he denounces the new government, relieves Gen. Hudson Austin of command, and calls on the people to arm themselves and rise against the villains of the Central Committee, who are now hiding out at Fort Frederick. The assembled multitude think this is a good idea until several of the armored cars supplied by the friendly Soviets come out of Fort Fred and open up on the crowd with automatic weapons. Chaos understandably results when the vehicles crash right into the crowd, killing about fifty people. The soldiers emerge from the APCs, grab the prime minister, and shoot him and his associates. General Austin declares the civil government dissolved, establishes martial law, and declares himself the ruling authority. The medical students keep to their dorm rooms and worry.

As a precaution, the American Joint Chiefs of Staff begin a "planning cycle." The same day, it so happens, the marines of Amphibious Squadron Four leave for Lebanon. A noncombat rescue of the students is considered.

Previous pages: Grenada, 1983. A trooper with a M203 participates in a real world exercise.

The next day, 20 October, a twenty-four-hour, shoot-on-sight curfew is put into effect on the island. The Special Situation Group is convened by Vice-president George Bush. The prime minister of Barbados requests the United States to intervene with military force. The battle group including the aircraft carrier *Independence* is diverted from its course toward Lebanon to Grenada, just in case. Amphibious Squadron Four is diverted to Grenada, just in case. The USSR recognizes and congratulates the new government; Cuba expresses reservations and concerns.

On 21 October, the neighboring countries of the Organization of Eastern Caribbean States (Antigua/Barbuda, Dominica, St. Kitts/Nevis, St. Lucia, St. Vincent/Grenadines, and Montserrat) plus Jamaica and Barbados ask for American participation in a joint military operation; they are planning to send their tiny forces and they want help. News of the conference is leaked to the Grenadians, Soviets, and Cubans. The Cuban government orders its troops on Grenada to begin defensive preparations. Serious planning for an operation by United States forces begins.

On 22 October, an American diplomatic mission is sent to the island, by an administration with memories of the hostages taken by Iran, in an effort to find a way to extract the Americans from the island. Although Austin had assured the students that they could leave at any time, none were permitted to depart. The two diplomats couldn't get answers from the officials they met, and concluded that there was no real government in place. The president now approves a military contingency plan—an endorsement that allows preparation but not execution.

On 23 October, captive Grenadian Governor General Sir Paul Scoon smuggles out a message asking for American military intervention, *quickly*. On the island, the Cubans insert a colonel and his security team and transmit a message: "Expect no reinforcements." The Cubans begin to take charge, helping the Grenadians dig in and site automatic weapons. The runway at Point Salines is blocked.

At 1700 hours on 23 October, President Reagan signs the orders authorizing the execution of the mission. Strategic objectives: safety of American citizens, restoration of democratic government, elimination of Cuban influence. D day will be 25 October, H hour 0500. It will be a joint air-sea-land operation. Civilian casualties among the population must be kept to an absolute minimum.

On 24 October, Cuban Col. Pedro Tortolo takes command of the military forces on the island. President Reagan meets with the Joint Chiefs of Staff. The unified commander of the forces will be Adm. Wesley McDonald, who creates something called Joint Task Force 120. He will be the theater commander and liaison between the assaulting elements and Washington. The commander of JTF 120 is Adm. Joseph Metcalf III, who specified the objectives for the elements of the force. Army, navy, marine, and air force planners prepare for the curtain to go up on an opening night instead of another rehearsal. They are designing a performance with thousands of actors and billions of dollars worth of props and sets—a drama in one act for the audience of world opinion and world politics. They know the death scenes will be real, but they will not know who lives and dies until the curtain falls. It is the highest form of drama. N hour has come and gone, the eighteen-hour sequence has run its course, the wheels have come up on the first aircraft. It is 0001 on 25 October 1983.

Getting ready to go, but for real this time.

The assault begins well before dawn with Navy SEALs coming ashore to prepare for the invasion. They paddle silently in small teams and go to work. Several promptly die.

At 0300, the Spectre gunships arrive on station and begin their methodical racetrack flight pattern over the Point Salines airport.

H hour is supposed to be 0500, but it is missed when navigational gear on the lead bird decides to go "bravo delta."

At 0520, the marines land by helicopter at Pearls Airport on the northern side of the island and by amphibious assault at the capital city of St. George's.

At 0536, as night becomes day, the army's two Ranger battalions, 1st and 2nd of the 75th Infantry (Airborne, Ranger) begin the assault onto the strip the Cubans were building at Point Salines.

The Rangers see that they will take a lot of heat from the Cubans' antiaircraft weapons, well sited to put fire on planes flying at drop altitude — 1250 feet. The decision is made to go down to 500 feet, below the line of fire of most of the 23mm "trip-A," as antiaircraft artillery is called. The Cubans take them under heavy and effective fire from several batteries, one of which locks on to the leader. The jumpers in the lead aircraft, including a command section, a combat control team, and Companies Alpha and Bravo, 1st of the 75th Rangers, step out into the warm air before the command to abort can be given, and float down for thirty seconds while the defenders greet them with small-arms fire. They find themselves alone and forsaken on the hot concrete drop zone for fifteen minutes that seem like an eternity. They huddle behind whatever cover they can find, something Rangers are loath to do, and swear, something at which they excel.

The Air Force Spectre gunship begins to hose the defenders with its heavy metal magic. The jump aircraft return to a quieter airspace and let the gunships earn their keep for a few minutes. Then, it is time to try it again: the aircraft line up on the DZ, make their runs through a more friendly sky, and eject their loads. The element of surprise seems to be lacking. The Rangers jump from 500 feet without reserves. The air force is supposed to slow down the planes to 130 knots during the jump, but several, anxious to escape the beaten zone over the two-mile DZ, do not. The Rangers land, get out of their harnesses, and scramble to extract weapons from their containers. They are well engaged by the defenders, who are ready and sometimes willing. At one point, two Rangers are pinned down fifteen meters from a member of the loyal opposition;

they call for fire support from the Spectre, which regretfully declines the invitation because of the small margin for error. "You shoot them, or they shoot us. Take your pick," is the Ranger reply. The Spectre fires, hammering the enemy into pulp, and the Rangers move out to establish the airhead. Some race toward the campus where half the Americans are hiding and as yet unaware of exactly what's going on. At 0850, the Rangers succeed in rescuing the first of the students. They move up to the campus through defensive positions established by the Cubans. A soldier in full camouflage bursts into the men's dorm: "American soldier!" he yells at the students. "We're here to take you home!"

The Rangers have brought two aliens with them — 82nd Airborne engineers who make the

---

82nd Airborne troopers apply camouflage paint to faces before operations on Grenada.

jump to clear the heavy construction vehicles the Cubans have been using as anti-invasion obstacles. For one of them, it is his "cherry" jump, the first jump after Benning. What is it like to jump from 500 feet into a hot LZ?

"It's too *high*, if you ask me," says one of the engineers. "I could see all over the island. You could see the people on the ground. They were running around, getting ammunition and getting into position. Two hundred feet would have been fine with me!"

He and the other engineer have the job of hot wiring the construction vehicles, a problem made more difficult because all the information on the gauges and switches is either in Spanish or Japanese. But they get them fired up, encouraged by the snap, crackle, and pop of bullets in the air overhead.

"I fired nine rounds from my M-16," one engineer reports. "There was a big plate glass window in one of the buildings that I was firing at, but I didn't hit it. Then a Cuban ran out the back, and I got off one shot at him, but I missed him, too."

The engineers may not be red-hot riflemen, but that's not why they're here. They're here to clear the runway of all the obstacles that have been planted in the pavement, and they get to it, using the construction equipment to push aside or flatten the stakes and barricades that prevent the strip from accepting aircraft. They soon have enough of it cleared for the big jets to land, if they will do it one at a time, and the word goes out to the airborne commander, who makes the decision: "Airland the troops, no drop for the 82nd's part of the assault phase of the operation."

The runway is clear at 1000, and the airland operation begins. The platoon leader of the lead element from the 82nd says: *We were airlanded rather than airdropped; we didn't know what it would be until two hours out. We had parachutes in the aircraft. We didn't know the situation on the runway. General Trobaugh was with our platoon; we were the first plane. He had a TACSET and had communications with the Rangers on the ground. We based our plans on a set situation, but this situation was changing while we were in the air. As we were going down there he got the word that the runway was clear. Now, the runway was clear of obstructions—but it was not clear of the enemy! There was still enemy fire that could be directed on the runway.*

There is an advantage in control when you airland in that you get off the plane together, and you have a little more control initially, but the disadvantage was that the runway could only handle one C-141 at a time, so it took us longer to assemble our combat power on the ground by airlanding than if we jumped. Plus, we didn't get our gold star on our jump wings!

Another member of the lead element, a master sergeant, comments:

When we landed and when the tailgate went down, everybody was very anxious to get the fuck off the aircraft, because all anybody was thinking was: you're sitting in this big box filled with fuel. Almost everybody was crowded back around the tailgate, then the aircraft finally stopped and everybody exited. You could hear the crack of bullets overhead, and see the green tracers. That's when it really began to sink in: this is hostile! *You are being* shot *at!*

We ran over to a big ditch and assembled. The officers had a powwow to decide what to do next, then we began to move out. There in the pathway was a Cuban soldier who'd been stitched up the middle, lying there dead. And just further on, there were three other Cuban soldiers prone on the ground, being guarded by MPs, bawling like babies! And that was the first time it struck: this is really alien. This is a totally different thing than I have ever done before. That guy is dead over there. This is Big Time.

The Rangers had established and secured the airhead, but the job was not quite complete and would not be until the opposition no longer wanted to come out and fight. Bravo Company, 1st of the 75th, assaults toward the western end of the ridge while mortar rounds drop around them.

Their first sergeant and three of his Rangers charge into a Cuban platoon, kill two and capture twenty-eight. Their snipers take out the mortar gunners from 1,000 meters with rifle fire. The first sergeant convinces another 175 Cubans to surrender.

While the 82nd troops begin to move out and up the hill toward a Cuban compound, they link

Troops move past two Soviet BTR-60 armored cars, taken out with LAWs. Somebody has scored with a neat shot right on the driver's position, which penetrated the aluminum armor and the driver as well.

Flags honor a captain and sergeant from the 325th killed on this spot above Point Salines while doing a leader's recon.

up with the Rangers. Alpha Company, 2nd Battalion, 325th Airborne Infantry Regiment, is working with one of the Ranger companies when three armored personnel carriers—Russian-built BTR-60s—emerge from the jungle and begin attacking the infantry at the same time that fire from the Calliste compound, their objective, begins to fall on them. The armor is on the Ranger side of the formation and scares the socks off just about everybody. It is the right move at the right place; the Cuban who leads the force to this opportunity, Capt. Sergio Grandales-Nolasco, puts his force in a position to inflict a great deal of harm to the budding assault. The infantry is designed for rapid movement, not slugfests with armor, and is lightly armed. But it is not defenseless, either; the Rangers have old 90mm recoilless rifles, dis-

carded by most of the rest of the ground forces, who now use TOW missiles. The missile systems are heavier and slower, though, and the Rangers have stuck with the old weapon. They also have a good supply of LAWs, the light antiarmor/fortification rocket that is freely dispensed to the infantry. The LAW is not effective against a main battle tank, but it will put a hole in the lighter armor that goes on a BTR. And that's exactly what they do. For a few moments, it is up for grabs as the BTRs fire hot and heavy with their 14.5mm heavy machine guns. A Ranger lieutenant grabs a LAW and prepares to fire, but is cut down by the machine gun's fire. Everyone in range begins to cut loose on the three moving targets. The 90mm rifles begin to speak and find the range on the lead BTR, which lurches to a stop, fatally wounded. The second and third BTRs also come under fire; number two is slain and the sole survivor turns to escape back to the tree line, small arms fire bouncing from its aluminum hide. The crews of the two wrecked vehicles come out and fall, dead or wounded. A Spectre gunship finds the escaping BTR and brings its heavy artillery to bear on the sole survivor, firing four 105mm rounds at the target and bringing it to a sudden halt.

The two companies continue the assault up toward Calliste, which has grown quiet after the incident with the armor. The company commander and a sergeant move forward to do a "leader's recon" before bringing the company up. A machine gun opens up from a well-designed ambush and both die; they are replaced and the assault continues. The objective is taken.

The Rangers are relieved effective 1900 hours on 25 October and go home. Fighting continues at a diminishing pace as the defense crumbles and surrenders or dies. All the students are rescued.

The patrols go out and the blood adrenaline levels decline. At last, it is over and everybody stops to consider the event. The troops evaluate it; the American people evaluate it; the Cubans, Soviets, Bulgarians, and other members of the OPFOR evaluate it.

One of the surprises was that the population of the nation we invaded seemed genuinely grateful and liberated . . . just as we had hoped. In many ways, it was a victory even more satisfying than just beating the other side. The howls of protest from the American and foreign press were muted by the expressions of delight from the students and the Grenadians. The whole exercise was pulled off with little loss of life and property all the way around. The major casualties were to the pride and image of the Cubans and the Soviet bloc nations. The huge caches of weapons and ammunition found around the island by the patrols were far in excess of anything the Grenadians needed for any purpose—except export. The Cubans, both living and dead, were shipped back to where they had come from. The Russians left, too, after the weapons were removed from their luggage. Their credibility on Third World issues was severely damaged by the whole encounter. Colonel Tortolo and several of his aides managed to escape capture, although perhaps they wish they hadn't. Castro rewarded Tortolo with an all-expenses-paid trip to Angola as a private soldier.

It wasn't black, and it wasn't white, but wars never really are. Was it a proper use of American military power? Was it just a giant squashing some insignificant bug? Was it a clumsy and ill-considered adventure by an establishment that had nothing better to do? While the politicians and news and opinion papers had their say, the troops tried to evaluate the significance of it all. In some

One of the OPFOR in custody of the military police.

ways, the questions of policy and politics and world opinion should not matter to a soldier; a soldier is supposed to follow orders. But American soldiers are supposed to follow *lawful* orders, and for them, these things are important and do count. American soldiers require of their leaders—from squad leader to commander in chief—that they be worthy of trust. They accept the possibility that their lives may be spent in the national interest, but they insist that the national interest be truly and properly at risk. Nineteen American soldiers died, 115 were wounded. Was it worth it? The consensus seems to be that it was.

THE LESSONS OF "URGENT FURY"

The leaders of the platoons and companies have given a great deal of thought to the professional details of the way they executed the operation, how it worked, what went well and what went wrong. They learned a lot and are still applying the lessons. It changed the way the 82nd does business. Here is what some of the platoon and company leaders say.

One of the senior NCOs of the lead element describes the hours after notification:

It didn't really sink in until we were well into the eighteen-hour sequence that it was a real-world alert and we were going someplace. There was a much different atmosphere. But we didn't get the word until quite late that it wasn't just another EDRE. We got all the extra weapons out of the Arms Room. What struck me was, everybody behaved the way they were trained. You didn't have anybody going off the deep end or AWOL or anything. We got to the Corps Holding Area (ammunition issue point) before the guys with the keys. We call 'em "cosmonauts" around here, the "legs" that run the vans with the ammunition and stuff on them. We were speeded up in our eighteen-hour sequence because we didn't have time, we had to get the fuck out of here, and we beat the guys with the keys down there. We were waiting to go before the equipment got there. If it hadn't been for the guys with the keys and some little stuff like that, we could have loaded a lot earlier than we did.

We were the Mortar Platoon, and we learned a lot about how to configure the equipment so that it will arrive at the same time you do. We learned the importance of making sure you have the means of moving ammunition around once you get there. We had a hundred and ten rounds of HE and no way to get it from here to there. We ended up getting an engineer dump truck to take us to our first position, and we had to commandeer a Cuban vehicle for the rest of the time. We learned a lot tactically down there we hadn't realized before. One of the key lessons we learned was: you've gotta be flexible! I don't care how good your plans are. We've got a big package of up-loaded equipment which is supposed to go on the airplane; but when the time came, there weren't enough airplanes for all the vehicles and equipment, so we went down there and had nothing except whatever we could steal.

And the important thing is that at nine o'clock the night before, everyone had been at home watching Monday Night Football, and at two in the afternoon of the following day we were in a combat environment!

The platoon leader:

We never received a full-blown plan. What I got as a platoon leader was that the situation was changing constantly, and that initially we were going to assemble on the northern side of the runway at this location, and they showed it to me on an aerial photograph that I was then able to show to all my men, and then we'll move out from there and tentatively we'll have a blocking position here at the edge of the runway. Great.

But that just went out the window as soon as we got off the plane. We ran to the side of the runway. A ranger colonel drove up in a Cuban truck and waved down my commander and said: "The Rangers are up there. Go link up with them!" And so we moved up and linked up with the Rangers. And, slowly, as the rest of our company arrived on subsequent aircraft, we worked out around the southern side of the Cuban compound where we could orient our fires and clear the buildings to our rear. We met the major opposition on the island.

We never had to mount a deliberate attack on this compound because the A-7s and the M-60 machine gun fire that we placed on it effectively convinced them to surrender before we had to close with them.

Our M-60s got some good licks in on the compound. The range was five or six hundred meters, so it wasn't effective small arms range. But, as a matter of fact, some of the guys were firing their M-203s into the compound and hitting the fringes of it, and exploded some ammunition stored there. Then BRAVO company was given the mission to circle around and get on the north side of the compound and that's when Captain Ritz was killed there. Then, the next day, the whole area was reduced, after the A-7s made it through. After that, it was mainly searching.

There was a Marine roadblock, and houses right across the street that we found weapons in, that these Marines had never looked in!

The Cubans, by the time we arrived, their organization had pretty much broken down as a result of the shock of the Ranger assault. What you had was fragmented groups of Cubans running around, two or three at a time, with their AKs, firing on groups, and the actions that did develop were real small. Two or three guys shooting, returning fire. So there was never a case where I could say, "There's a dug in Cuban squad! I'm gonna do the FM-7 dash 8 attack." It just didn't exist. We did use movement-to-contact formations, but the enemy was elusive in the sense that they were firing from houses, disappearing.

We captured three Cubans. They were hiding in a house that the Rangers told us was cleared. We moved down there, and I was lying there with my platoon, with our backs to the house . . . and, well, I'll never make THAT mistake again! This Grenadian guy runs out of the house and over to me and says, "There are Cubans in my house!"

So everyone locks and loads on the house and these three guys come out, and they were kind of smiling. So I asked one of my Spanish speaking soldiers to tell them to lay down. He said something to them—I don't know what it was—but they were begging for their lives! Then, when we started to move them back to turn them into the MPs, their compadres down the hill saw that they were trying to surrender and tried to kill them. We were within range of each other, and they fired up at us, and everybody hit the ground. So I said, "This is interesting." So I had them stand up again, and they started firing again! That's right, they were shooting at their buddies! We had them low-crawl from there back to the POW collection point. Those guys were kind of happy to be captured; but there were some who were trying to be hardcore.

I guess the thing about Grenada, though, that made it different than any other conflict, was that it came on with absolutely no notice, especially for the 82nd. We received less notice than anybody else. The thing that impressed me the most about the way things happened was that we took these troops, these eighteen- and nineteen-year-old kids right out of the barracks, and in eighteen hours threw them into a combat situation. It impressed the hell out of me that we could take these kids on a typical Monday night and threw them into a combat situation and they did a hell of a good job!

Epilogue:
Push Comes to Shove

Thinking and writing about the military during these isolationist times goes against the grain of popular American thought. We, as a nation, don't read much history or think much about how the past foretells the future. We are, and have been from the beginning, a pretty pacifist lot, happy to be left alone with our space and our resources. But time and circumstance have intersected with regularity over the preceding two hundred and umpteen years, and Americans have decided to send young men off to mortal combat. Sometimes the conflicts have been big and substantial, sometimes small and dubious. And, it seems, after every war the lessons are forgotten and we say, "This will never happen again."

I am sorry to be the bearer of sad tidings, but I think that it *will* happen again, and it makes a lot of sense to be ready. Twenty-one times in the past four decades, major airborne operations have been mounted and executed against a hostile force. Twenty-one times the people who command the commanders have decided that it is time to lock and load a battalion or a brigade or more of these fine young men, and they are ordered off, sometimes to be extinguished in mortal combat. Their lives are spent to buy some measure of control of the world we live in. During the Grenada operation, nineteen Americans died and 115 were wounded. Compared to other conflicts, that was a small price to pay—unless you happened to have been one of the dead or wounded. My point is that the cost of maintaining a military is always expensive, one way or another. Neglecting the military during the 1920s and 1930s cost hundreds of thousands (perhaps millions) of lives in the 1940s.

We owe it to these men that if we have to spend their lives in our collective interest, we must be very careful about how, when, where, and why we do it. And as expensive as war and warriors may be, they are a better bargain than some of the things that pass for peace.

But we will have to spend some of them again, sooner or later. In a month, or a year, or a decade, someplace, somehow, push once more will come to shove, and the people we elect to govern us all will stay up late and struggle with the sit-reps, the intel reports, and the issues. They will reach difficult decisions. The people who command the commanders will sign the orders and make the calls on the secure telephone lines. For the twenty-second time, the documents will begin: "THIS IS AN EXECUTE ORDER, BY AUTHORITY AND DIRECTION OF THE SECRETARY OF DEFENSE." In the N Plus Two room, the leaders will assemble in their multitudes, in full camouflage and burdened with their load-bearing equipment. They will hear the general's aide announce, "Gentlemen, the division commander!" The jumpmasters will load their sticks at Green Ramp, the troops will file into the cavernous planes. Sometime before eighteen hours have elapsed, an air force pilot will ease forward the four throttles and a bird will climb into the air and suck up its gear, shaping a course for someplace far away. Then, all too soon, tracers will slice the night and the nation will again command, "STAND UP!" and "HOOK UP!" and "STAND IN THE DOOR!"

Previous pages: Two members of a fire team from A Company, 2nd Battalion, 325th Airborne Infantry Regiment. *Right:* Teamwork is everything, even when you drop by the MOUT site for a visit.

The Inventory

The airborne requires many physical resources to go about its business: parachutes of various sizes and sorts, small arms and heavy weapons, helicopters and ground vehicles, and a multitude of other costly resources, many of which are important or necessary for the successful completion of the missions with which the organizations are tasked. These resources are worth consideration if you're interested in understanding the capabilities and limitations of the organization.

The army is built on its people, and the whole army, navy, and air force really exist to support one kind of people—infantrymen. Their MOS (military occupational specialty) is called "eleven bravo," the designation for a basic rifleman trooper. They've been called all sorts of names over the years, from "dogface" to "grunt," but the operative term in the Army of Excellence is eleven bravo.

In the 82nd, the average age of these troopers is twenty-four, if you include everybody. Among the troops in the infantry platoons, it's more like twenty-two. With rare exceptions, they are high school graduates; a large percentage have attended college. The average IQ is above average (108). Each trooper runs about 600 miles a year, and almost every one is a qualified parachutist. There are about a hundred of them in each infantry company. They have a sense of humor and a kind of tribal affinity for each other, like members of some highly select fraternity, which, of course, they are. They spend a lot of time in the field and have learned how to live there with a certain amount of comfort and style.

They have developed a kind of language that is (once you get used to it) funny, bawdy, and charming. It is also quite obscene. It is seasoned by so much profanity that the profane words have been drained of any profane intent, and they cease to have any connections with the acts or objects they otherwise represent. If you could edit out the obscenities of soldiers' speech, the meaning would usually be unchanged. There are exceptions, and they are usually humorous. In fact, there is a great deal of sophisticated humor within this society, but much of it defies translation out of context. When your life is available to be spent as needed by people you don't know, and who routinely require you to do all manner of tiring and seemingly useless activities, you either find a way of accepting it or you go someplace else. One way of accepting it is to convert it to humor, mixing and matching formal military jargon with a wry and cynical point of view; thus a person who insists on being consistently wrong is "spring-loaded in the dumb position."

T10 PARACHUTE/ MC1-1B PARACHUTE

These are the two basic personnel static line parachutes used by airborne soldiers. They are similar, with the exception that the latter has the ability to be steered. They are parabolic in cross section, which means that the skirt is ten feet smaller than the widest part of the canopy. These parachutes seem not greatly different than the T4 parachute developed in 1940, but the nature of the materials used in construction, and several innovations over the years, make them far more reliable, safe, and comfortable for the jumper.

The T-10, a 34-foot parabolic parachute with anti-inversion net.

They still work in the same basic way: as the jumper falls away from the aircraft, the yellow static line extends to its full fifteen-foot length, at which point the tension on the static line breaks the first piece of string that holds the whole thing together—the pack closing tie. The static line now holds the deployment bag while the jumper continues to fall away; two other ties that secure the connector links break and the suspension lines start to run out of the stow loops on the deployment bag. The last of these unlocks the canopy from the bag and it extends, skirt first. The jumper is still connected to the aircraft, although he's about forty feet below and behind it now. When the canopy is fully extended, the final tie breaks that connects the static line to the apex of the canopy; the canopy begins to inflate. The opening time for either the T10 or the MC1-1B

varies with the speed of the aircraft, ranging from about seven seconds (from a helicopter doing 60 knots) to about two seconds from a C-130 or -141 (doing 130 knots).

Parachutes used to open with a jolt that would knock your socks off. The canopy began to inflate before the suspension lines had fully extended, with the result that the jumper fell about thirty feet and then stopped, bang. Jumpers were often bruised and sometimes rendered unconscious. But the rapid deployment saved lives when the jump altitude was 175 feet, as it was at Noemfoor Island on New Guinea in 1944.

Parachutes also used to be subject to a variety of malfunctions: streamers, inversions, and blown panels were once rather common. There are still malfunctions, but they are exceedingly rare, thanks in part to the invention of deployment bags but also to the addition to the canopy of an anti-inversion net.

Today's parachutes are safer and more comfortable. The old T4 had a canopy that was only twenty-eight feet in diameter and a rate of descent faster than today's T10 with its much larger canopy. The T10 can be maneuvered by hauling down on the risers and spilling air out from one side of the canopy or the other, but it is a limited kind of steering.

The MC1-1B, on the other hand, is the sporty model, and you can zip around over the DZ like a maniac if you need to. It uses toggle lines running up to the vents in the back of the canopy; pulling on a toggle line closes one of the vents a little and the whole rig pivots. You can turn a full 360 degrees in 8.8 seconds (unless you get caught by a Black Hat first). The vents also give the canopy forward motion—about fourteen feet per second. This is a fairly handy feature if you're high enough

125

to get any benefit from it; you can "fly" over toward your assembly point and save yourself part of the hike, or move away from other jumpers in the air. Airborne students make two jumps with this parachute, but they are not likely to use it much after that. Almost everybody in the 82nd jumps with the good old T10.

M-16 RIFLE

The M-16 has been around since the 1950s, and made its debut in the combat zone in 1963. It was a radical notion of weapon design at the time, and it still looks pretty futuristic. It is light and was sometimes called the "plastic rifle" by the troops. It used a much smaller bullet than was previously thought necessary, and that little bullet was pumped up to very high velocities. It could shoot "full auto," which means that you could spray all thirty of the bullets in your magazine into the air over the head of the guy you're trying to kill, all at once without even trying, and scare him to death. Previously, you had to aim and fire one shot at a time, with the risk that you might hurt somebody.

Not long after the rifle was tested and approved for use by the troops, somebody decided to change the kind of powder that was used in the cartridges; instead of going "bang" at critical moments, the rifle was merely going "click." Click is not the sound you want your rifle to make while having a disagreement with the guys from Brand X. The survivors complained to the management; the management replied that *if* there was a problem, it was because the troops weren't cleaning their rifles and it was their own damn fault. This led to all manner of arm waving, but some modifications were finally made and by the time the war

The M-16A1, the "plastic rifle."

was lost, the bugs were worked out and the basic weapon of the infantryman worked well.

It works even better now in the M-16A2 version, recently released and available at your local arms room. The A2 has a three-shot burst capability, which helps conserve ammunition while still putting some serious lead downrange. The stock is a little longer, so it fits most people better. It has a lot of little improvements that make it more reliable and accurate.

Although the bullet will carry for many hundreds of meters, the army says the effective combat range of the M-16 is about 200 meters; this means that if you try to get off an aimed shot at a man-sized target 200 meters away, you have a 50:50 probability of hitting it somewhere or other.

M-203 DUAL-PURPOSE WEAPON

This is a combination of a standard rifle onto

126

which has been grafted a single-shot grenade launcher. The grenade launcher uses 40mm cartridges that come in several varieties—high explosive, smoke, flare, tear gas—and are handy particularly when people you don't like are just over that little hill 100 meters to the front. Then, you can lob your 40mm messages over where no rifle or machine gun can reach, and anybody within fifteen meters of the point of impact will wish you hadn't done that. There are two M-203s in a squad, and they are a short-range version of artillery, providing indirect fire when nothing else will do. The M-203 replaces the old M-79 grenade launcher, which resembled a shotgun that had been run through the washer and dryer and emerged badly shrunk and warped. But it sure was handy in Viet Nam. Occasionally it was used with "beanbag" projectiles to stun one of the enemy without killing him; then Charles would be taken back to the intel team at Camp Swampy for a little chat.

The Belgian-designed squad automatic weapon (SAW).

SQUAD AUTOMATIC WEAPON

This is a light machine gun, designed in Belgium, which was adopted by the army in 1982. The idea was to provide each of the four squads of an infantry platoon with an effective bullet hose for those critical moments in a young man's life— those moments when nothing but industrial strength threats and intimidation are required. You know, as when you have to assault a well-defended position and there are thirty or forty guys on the other team shooting at you. That's when you want the good old M-249 SAW. It will crank out 750 of those little 5.56mm zippers every minute you can keep it fed, and even more if you flip the switch to "adverse." It will throw its greetings out to 3,600 meters, although it is only supposed to be effective to 1,000. It is supposed to be able to use the same magazine the M-16 uses, but there are some problems with that. But the troops like the beast. It's a lot lighter, at fifteen pounds,

M-203 rifle and grenade launcher.

The SAW isn't the most accurate weapon on the battlefield, but machine guns are seldom used for sniping. It tends to throw its groups vertically, which is unfortunate but acceptable. SAWs are used for spraying an area and controlling a field of fire. The area it shoots at is called the "beaten zone," and it is not a happy place.

VULCAN AIR DEFENSE SYSTEM

As the British discovered on the Falklands, enemy air can ruin the party for the infantry, and an effective defense is necessary for a happy ending. The Vulcan is a modern version of the old Gatling gun, and there are forty-eight in the division. They fire from one thousand to three thousand 20mm bullets a minute at targets in the air or on the ground; a built-in radar helps aim the beast, correcting for lead angle. The Vulcan falls out of airplanes and rides around beneath helicopters to go where the action is.

COBRA HELICOPTER

The Cobra and the new Apache attack helicopters are the army's dependable air cover. They are designed to be tank busters in a large way and are likewise effective against troops. The Cobra will do 170 knots; has a range of 410 kilometers; and carries eight TOWs, two rocket pods, and a cannon. A grenade launcher and a minigun can also be used.

The Apache is more of the same but faster, with a new missile system, more armor, and better sights. It can fire a laser-homing missile at a target it can't even see, allowing a troop on the battlefield to mark the victim with a laser designator. The

Cobra helicopter, the army's reliable jet fighter.

than the old M-60 (that weighed twenty-three pounds dry and was sometimes called "The Pig"), which keeps the gunner feeling cheerful and refreshed after a hard day on the assault.

Ammunition is available in a variety of packages, the favorite being the 200-round "assault pack," a plastic box of convenient size and shape that is discarded when empty. The current one is green, and it has been suggested that it would be nice if it were transparent, so you could see what you have left. There has been some whining about the assault pack coming off the gun when the gunner hits the deck; the reply is that if the gunner falls correctly, the magazine isn't going to hit anything.

128

Apache is equipped with two engines and can haul an amazing quantity of ordnance on its stubby winglets.

105mm HOWITZER

Of all of the things that go bump in the night, nothing is more effective at killing people than artillery. The M-101A1 howitzer and its other mutations have been backing up the troops since 1939, and now defend more than fifty different nations, sometimes from each other. Each can bang away at the rate of 180 rounds an hour, but you need a good supply officer to keep that up for long. The bullets (you can call them projectiles if you must, but the battery commander says "bullets") will float out to 11,200 meters. That's about seven miles. If you get the chance, lie on the ground in front of a 105 that's firing at something far away, and gaze into the air where the bullet will go. You can watch the flight of the four-inch projectile—a dot that arcs up and away into the

Preparing to fire a LAW—light antitank weapon.

void until you lose sight of it. After a while— twenty seconds or so—a rumble that sounds like distant thunder can be heard from the other side of the mountain.

The 105 is capable of all sorts of handy chores. It can fire illumination rounds to help defeat a night attack, white phosphorous to burn, smoke to obscure, and leaflets to amuse the enemy. But when the going really gets tough and a battalion of bad guys is coming through the wire at you, all thoughts turn toward the "gun bunnies" and their supply of beehive rounds. Then, when no one else can save you, the 105 can sing of salvation; the bang of the gun is followed by an awful howl as thousands of tiny steel darts—a cloud of tiny killers—scream through the air at the attackers.

LAW

They call it the "light antitank weapon." Unfortunately, nobody uses light tanks anymore. It has been around for a couple of decades, having replaced the old 3.5-inch rocket launcher. The LAW fires a little rocket with a shaped charge warhead. It's light enough that anybody can carry one, and some get several. They are really most useful against buildings and fortifications that resist bullets. They will work against light armor and vehicles from 200 meters or so—when they work. At Lang Vei, when the North Vietnamese tanks overran the Special Forces compound, a few of the defenders tried to zap the tanks with LAWs. If the LAWs would have fired, the tanks (they were light tanks) would probably have been defeated; but the weapons didn't work, not one of the many that they tried. The camp was completely overrun. The few survivors made it out and back to Khe Sanh. The new LAWs are reputed to work better.

Abridged Dictionary of Airborne Terms, Slang, & Unconventional English

ARP: "Airborne Rifle Platoon," the scouts who operate in small groups out in front of the FEBA, setting up ambushes and reconning for the main units.

BDU: Battle Dress Utility, the normal work uniform used in the field.

BRAVO DELTA: "Broke Dick," a piece of hardware that doesn't work. "We had a jump scheduled for this morning, but the goddamn bird was bravo delta."

DSL: "Dangerous Sperm Load," a condition resulting from being out in the field and away from your sweetie for longer than twenty-four hours.

DUMMY CORD: OD green suspension line used to secure many of the items of equipment that get clipped to the Load Bearing Equipment (or LBE as they call it); the canteens, magazine cases, knives, and other bits and pieces of personal equipment have a way of working loose and falling off in sneaky ways.

FAST MOVER: air force air support aircraft, the jets that zoom above the battlefield putting out fires, typically A-10s, F-14s, and F-15s.

FEBA: "Forward Edge of Battle Area," the limit of advance or the approximate area where the meat grinder is at work.

FIDO: "Fuck It, Drive On!" An abbreviated suggestion to overcome an obstacle to progress and get on with the program. A company commander might snivel and whine to his battalion commander over the radio about why he is not making much progress in his mission, to which he will perhaps hear "FIDO!" as the entire response.

FLUFF AND BUFF: the new uniform standard in the AOE, meaning wash-and-wear, fluff-dried BDUs (as opposed to the traditional heavily starched and pressed uniforms of the past, with creases sharp enough to shave with) and buff-polished boots (as opposed to the spit-shined, glittering footwear of the past).

FUBAR: "Fucked Up Beyond All Recognition."

GOATSCREW: a variation on FUBAR, but not quite so bad. A disorganized, embarrassing, and graceless chaos.

GOOD TO GO: prepared for departure, mission ready.

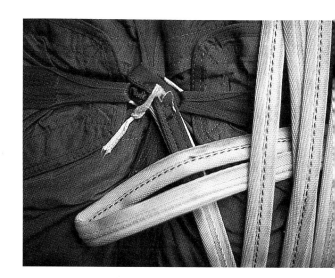

GUN BUNNY, FUSE LIGHTER: an artilleryman or a "thirteen bravo."

HARDCORE: professional attitude, a willingness to tolerate extreme hardship and adversity, going the extra mile on willpower alone. The guy who holds out when others are ready to quit.

HEARTBEAT: a basic measure of time.

HEARTBURN: anxiety, distress.

HIGH AND TIGHT: the most popular and trendy hairstyle among the troops; not quite shaved on the sides, with about a half-inch on top.

HIGH SPEED/LOW DRAG, sometimes HIGH SPEED LEFTWING LOW DRAG: applied to people as well as equipment. Highly mission ready; efficient; capable.

LEG: anyone in the military who is *not* Airborne qualified. An expletive.

MRE: officially, "Meal, Ready to Eat"; unofficially, "Meal, Rejected by Everyone." The new dehydrated combat meals that replaced the heavier old C rations (that were referred to as "C Rats").

NOTIONAL: imaginary, usually for the purposes of training.

SMOKE, THE CHIEF OF HEAT: the NCO in charge of an artillery firing battery.

SNIVEL, WHINE: complaining about the injustice of your allotted share. "I had to go over to the commander and do some serious sniveling to get those extra weapons."

SQUIGG: a practical joke.

TACTICAL: professional behavior or appearance. Sunglasses are not "tactical."

TOOTH-TO-TAIL RATIO: a comparison between the productive part of an organization (or in this case, the destructive part) and the supply system that sustains it; a notional measure of efficiency.

UMPTEENHUNDRED: sometime in the distant future, not yet determined.

"BLOOD UPON THE RISERS"*

"Is everybody happy?"
   cried the sergeant, looking up.
Our hero feebly answered "yes,"
   and then they stood him up.
He leaped right out into the blast,
   his static line unhooked,
And he ain't gonna jump no more!

He counted long, he counted loud,
   he waited for the shock.
He felt the wind, he felt the clouds,
   he felt the awful drop.
He jerked his cord, the silk spilled out
   and wrapped around his legs,
And he ain't gonna jump no more!

The risers wrapped around his neck,
   connectors cracked his dome.
The lines were snarled and tied in knots
   around his skinny bones.
The canopy became his shroud,
   he hurtled to the ground,
And he ain't gonna jump no more!

The days he'd lived and loved and laughed
   kept running through his mind.
He thought about the girl back home,
   the one he left behind.
He thought about the medics,
   and he wondered what they'd find,
And he ain't gonna jump no more!

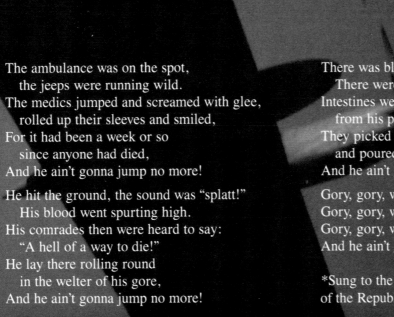

The ambulance was on the spot,
   the jeeps were running wild.
The medics jumped and screamed with glee,
   rolled up their sleeves and smiled,
For it had been a week or so
   since anyone had died,
And he ain't gonna jump no more!

He hit the ground, the sound was "splatt!"
   His blood went spurting high.
His comrades then were heard to say:
   "A hell of a way to die!"
He lay there rolling round
   in the welter of his gore,
And he ain't gonna jump no more!

There was blood upon the risers,
   There were brains upon the 'chute.
Intestines were a danglin'
   from his paratrooper's boots.
They picked him up still in his chute
   and poured him from his boots,
And he ain't gonna jump no more!

Gory, gory, what a hell of a way to die,
Gory, gory, what a hell of a way to die,
Gory, gory, what a hell of a way to die,
And he ain't gonna jump no more!

*Sung to the tune of "The Battle Hymn
of the Republic"

John Kim

About the Author/Photographer

Hans Halberstadt is a writer, photographer, and corporate film producer who sometimes lives in San Jose, California, when he is recovering from trips to Fort Bragg and Honduras. Halberstadt spent three years in the U.S. Army, which included a year in Viet Nam where he was a helicopter gunner. That experience resulted in an abiding interest in life and death issues which influences most of his projects. Previous books include USCG: ALWAYS READY and STAINED GLASS: MUSIC FOR THE EYE; soon to be released are Presidio POWER Books on the Green Berets, Rangers, and the National Training Center.